P9-CMQ-479

THE SUPREME COURT

THE SUPREME COURT

DAVID F. FORTE

American Government Series

87³²
347.1
FoR

Blairsville Junior High School
Blairsville, Pennsylvania

Consulting Editor, Richard Darilek
Department of History
Herbert H. Lehman College
The City University of New York

Franklin Watts
New York | London | 1979

Cover photograph courtesy of: United Press International.

Cartoons courtesy of:

ROTHCO CARTOONS: (Ivey) frontispiece; (Ruge) p. 28; (Pierotti) p. 39; (Renault—Sacramento Bee, Cal.) p. 42; (Konopacki) p. 44; (Miller— News & Observer, Raleigh, N.C.) p. 71; (Graham—Arkansas Gazette, Little Rock) p. 77; (Rosen—Albany Times-Union, N.Y.) p. 84; (Margulies) p. 100;
Sidney Harris: pp. 4, 14, 24, 104.

Library of Congress Cataloging in Publication Data

Forte, David F
  The Supreme Court.

  (American Government series)
  Bibliography: p.
  Includes index.
  SUMMARY: Examines the Supreme Court, its role in American history, and its influence on American life and law through landmark cases.
  1. United States. Supreme Court—Juvenile literature. 2. United States—Constitutional law— Juvenile literature. [1. United States. Supreme Court. 2. United States—Constitutional law] I. Title.
KF8742.Z9F57   347'.73'26   78–24214
ISBN 0–531–02267–6

Copyright © 1979 by Franklin Watts, Inc.
All rights reserved
Printed in the United States of America
5 4 3 2 1

To my mother

CONTENTS

THE SUPREME COURT

CHAPTER ONE

The Supreme Court: An Overview

When Marco DeFunis graduated from college, his over-whelming desire was to be a lawyer. He applied to the University of Washington Law School in 1970 but was re-jected. The Law School told him, however, that he would have a better chance of admission if he reapplied the fol-lowing year.

During the next few months, DeFunis worked to save some money and in his spare time took some graduate courses. He also studied hard to prepare himself to take the Law School Aptitude Test (LSAT) once again.

When he applied once again for admission to the Uni-versity of Washington Law School in early 1971, he was in a much stronger position. He had received nearly all A's in his graduate courses, and his last LSAT score was high. Nonetheless, the Law School did not accept DeFunis but placed him near the bottom of the waiting list. Toward the

"Before I took this job I never realized that we don't get any of that cops-and-robbers stuff."

end of the summer, the Law School's admissions committee informed him that he was once again rejected.

This was the last straw for DeFunis. He believed he was rejected because he was white. The Fourteenth Amendment to the United States Constitution forbids any state from denying "the equal protection of the laws" to persons within its jurisdiction. DeFunis took his case to court, charging that the State of Washington was guilty of racial discrimination. He asked the court to order the Law School to admit him.

During the trial it was revealed that the University of Washington Law School had received 1,601 applications for admission that session. The school had only 150 places available, but it had accepted 275 applicants, expecting that many would decide to go elsewhere.

Most of the students who applied were judged on their LSAT scores and their grades in the last two years of college. If an applicant's combined average was 77 or above, acceptance was practically certain. If the average was below 74.5, the applicant was usually rejected immediately. DeFunis' score was 76.23.

Minority students (for example blacks, Chicanos, and American Indians) were treated differently, however. Their applications were considered separately and not as much attention was paid to their scores. Of the 37 minority students who were accepted, 36 had scores below DeFunis' score, and 30 had an average below 74.5—the level at which most other students would have been automatically rejected.

State courts have the same right to interpret the federal Constitution that federal courts do. The trial court agreed with DeFunis. It found that the State of Washington, through its Law School, had been guilty of racial discrimination. On September 22, 1971, the court ordered the Law School to admit DeFunis into its first-year class.

But the battle had only just begun. The Law School complied with the trial court's order, and DeFunis registered as a student. However, at the same time, the Law School appealed the decision to the Washington State supreme court. Being a higher court, the state supreme court could reverse the lower court's decision.

In most states, the appeal process takes a long time. This was true in the State of Washington. It was over a year later, in March 1973, when the state supreme court finally handed down its decision. By that time, DeFunis was already nearing the end of his second year at the Law School.

By a vote of 5 to 4, the Washington State supreme court reversed the trial court's decision. The majority said that discrimination *against* a minority was unconstitutional but that discrimination designed to *help* a minority was acceptable in this case. Therefore, the Law School could keep DeFunis from finishing his course of study if it wanted to. The four-man minority dissented strongly. They argued that the Constitution forbids all kinds of racial discrimination, whether it be against blacks or whites.

A state supreme court is the highest authority concerning its own state's laws. But if it interprets the *federal* Constitution, then the losing party may appeal the decision to the United States Supreme Court. Marco DeFunis immediately lodged his appeal, but he ran into a serious problem. The Supreme Court was in its summer recess. If DeFunis had had to wait until autumn for the Court to be in session again, he would not have been allowed to start his third year of law school. He might even have been told to leave right away.

Fortunately, there is a procedure to take care of this

kind of problem. The United States is divided into eleven judicial *circuits*. Each circuit is supervised by one federal Supreme Court Justice. Since there are only nine Supreme Court Justices, two Justices must take care of an extra circuit each. Justice William O. Douglas was the Justice who supervised the ninth circuit, which took in the State of Washington.

When Justice Douglas received DeFunis' appeal, he ordered a *stay* in the Washington supreme court's decision. This way, DeFunis would not be expelled from the Law School or prevented from registering for his final year because the United States Supreme Court had his appeal pending before it in the fall.

There are two ways to take a state court decision to the United States Supreme Court. One is by *appeal*.

Suppose, for example, a woman claims that she has been deprived of work with the state because the state employment law unfairly discriminates against women in violation of the Fourteenth Amendment to the federal Constitution. If the woman loses because the state court finds that the state law is constitutional, then she may take her case to the Supreme Court by appeal.

But appeals are not the most common procedure. The other, more frequent method is by *certiorari*. Certiorari allows for Supreme Court review in most other issues concerning the Constitution or federal law. The Court must review a case sent up on proper appeal if there is a substantial federal question involved. The Court only accepts a case sent up by certiorari if four Justices think the case is important enough to warrant consideration. But even in the case of an appeal, four Justices must first decide if there is "a substantial federal question" involved in the case.

In the autumn of 1973, the Supreme Court met to consider DeFunis' appeal. The Court decided that it was not a proper appeal, but that it would still hear the case on the basis of certiorari. On February 26, 1974, the Court heard the arguments of both sides, and on April 23, 1974, it handed down its decision.

The Court held that it would not decide the case at all. It said that the issue was *moot*—that is, no matter what they decided, DeFunis would be in the same position as before. Nothing would change. He was about to graduate from the Law School, and even if the Supreme Court upheld the policy of favoring minorities over whites, the Law School had promised not to expel DeFunis.

The Supreme Court requires that the parties who come before it have a real "case or controversy." The Court will not decide constitutional issues simply because they are interesting. It does not give advisory opinions. A party must show he is personally being harmed in the controversy. Unless the parties' positions can be changed by the Court's decision, the Court will refuse to render a judgment.

Justice William O. Douglas dissented from the Court's opinion. He asserted that the Law-School's selections must be based on "racially neutral" standards. Despite Douglas's objections, the Supreme Court sent the case back down to the Washington supreme court for final decision. (Often the Supreme Court *remands* a case back to a lower court for final disposition, in light of what the Court has decided.) Many observers believed that the Court had used the mootness argument to avoid being entangled in an emotional issue.

By the time the Washington supreme court looked at the case again, DeFunis had graduated. But he did not give up his attempt to win his legal point. He tried making the case into a *class action*. Sometimes a court will hear a case not because one person claims hurt but because that person represents a whole group of people in a similar situation. DeFunis argued that even though his own particular case was moot, he represented all students who had been rejected because of racial favoritism.

The Washington supreme court disagreed. Being a law graduate, DeFunis could no longer represent students trying to get into law school. The court reinstated its earlier decision. It held that the Law School admissions policy favoring minorities was constitutional. Although DeFunis had finished law school, he had lost his case.

Even though the Supreme Court had successfully dodged the DeFunis case, the issue of "reverse discrimination" would not go away. A few years later a man named Alan Bakke was refused admission to medical school. We shall review his case in Chapter Four of this book.

A NOTE ON COURT STRUCTURE

There are two parallel court structures in the United States: the state and the federal. Marco DeFunis began his case in the state courts, appealed to the highest federal court, and then had the final decision made once again by the state supreme court. Some states have two levels of courts, others three. In some states the judges are appointed, while in others the judges are elected. Many states also have specialized courts such as municipal, county, probate, surrogate, family, land, chancery, juvenile, and traffic courts.

The federal court system has three basic levels. At the base are at present eighty-nine *district courts*. They are spread throughout the fifty states, the District of Columbia, Guam, Puerto Rico, the Canal Zone, and the Virgin Islands. Most federal cases begin at the district level.

The district courts hear cases based on federal law, or financial suits between citizens of different states (when the amount sued for is over $10,000) .

At the next level are the *circuit courts of appeal.* The eleven circuit courts hear appeals from the district courts and from agencies in the federal bureaucracy. In early times, the Supreme Court Justices themselves used to hear appeals from the lower federal courts while "riding circuit." Nowadays, the circuit courts are staffed with their own judges, although, as we saw in the DeFunis case, the Supreme Court Justices retain certain supervisory powers. Circuit judges usually sit in panels of three to hear the appeals.

The *Supreme Court* is at the top of the structure. It can hear cases, by appeal or by certiorari, from the highest state courts or from the lower federal courts. (Lower federal courts, troubled by a specific legal issue, may also ask the Supreme Court "by certification" for a decision on a matter.) The Supreme Court is headed by a Chief Justice and eight Associate Justices. Congress sets the number of Supreme Court Justices. Originally there were six, but the number has remained at nine ever since 1869.

All federal judges at the district and Supreme Court levels are appointed by the President of the United States with the consent of the Senate. They serve for life on "good behavior." They may be impeached, as tradition has developed, only for serious crimes, and their salaries may not be reduced during their appointments.

These conditions were created to help keep the judges free from political control. They have also allowed the federal courts to be more independent and powerful in our society.

There are also, in the federal structure, a number of

specialized courts: (1) *The court of claims* hears cases lodged against the government. If a person believes the government owes him money, in many cases he can take his demand to the court of claims. This court has seven judges, usually sitting in panels of three judges for each case. The President appoints the judges for life with the consent of the Senate. The Supreme Court can review court of claims decisions. (2) *The customs court* hears cases contesting specific tariffs on imports. It has nine judges (no more than five from any political party), but they divide into panels of three (or sometimes even one) to hear each case. The judges serve for life. The court's decisions can be appealed to the court of customs and patent appeals. (3) As the name suggests, the *court of customs and patent appeals* hears appeals both from the customs court and from the patent office. The court consists of five judges appointed by the President with the consent of the Senate. Its decisions are reviewable by the Supreme Court. (4) The *tax court* is really part of the executive branch of the government. It hears cases brought by the Internal Revenue Service against taxpayers who are charged with owing taxes. It is not a criminal court. It decides only if certain tax payments are due or not. The President, with the consent of the Senate, appoints sixteen judges for terms of twelve years. As with other agencies in the executive branch (such as the Interstate Commerce Commission, the Securities and Exchange Commission, and many others), the tax court's decisions are reviewed by the circuit court of appeals.

CHAPTER TWO

The Establishment of Judicial Review

It was almost a natural instinct for Marco DeFunis and Alan Bakke to take their problems to the court system. In America we accept the notion that our courts have the final say. Congress, the President, the bureaucracy, state courts, and state legislatures can all be reviewed by a federal court. Our courts even supervise actions by school boards and hospital staffs. We give our courts great power. Americans generally believe that for every social ill, there is some court to cure it.

This is, of course, not entirely true. American courts, including the Supreme Court, operate under many limitations. Some of these limitations, such as constitutional amendments and public opinion, are imposed from outside the court system. Others concern the way courts handle issues. Nevertheless America, more than any other nation in the world, turns its problems into legal disputes.

No other nation gives so much power to its courts. Yet even in the United States, it was not clear at the beginning that the courts should have the power to review and possibly nullify actions of other parts of the government.

In Philadelphia in 1787, delegates met to write the Constitution. They were primarily concerned with the powers and the structure of Congress. Little attention was paid to the judiciary. Some delegates made brief mention of their opinion that the new Supreme Court should have an independent power to review acts of Congress. Men like Elbridge Gerry of Massachusetts and Luther Martin of Maryland were in favor of a strong court. But most of the other delegates seemed unconcerned.

The problem was that during the struggle for independence, America had developed two opposite viewpoints. On the one hand, the colonists were angry because the British Parliament had taken away from them traditional rights which the colonies had lived with for over a hundred years. Parliament, for example, had no representatives from America, and this led many Americans to believe that only legislatures with properly elected representatives ought to make laws.

On the other hand, America had already developed a long tradition of written constitutions, charters, and compacts. Americans believed that acts of Parliament which violated those charters were not valid. In fact, some prominent American patriots asserted that the courts could veto these "illegal" acts of Parliament. In 1761, for example, James Otis argued before a Massachusetts court that Parliament had no right to authorize the Writs of Assistance. These writs gave the King's agents the right to search ships for smuggled goods without a search warrant. Otis said that if the court found these acts contrary to reason and the traditional rights of the American colonists, they could be nullified.

Otis lost his case. The court in Massachusetts said that Parliament was supreme. Indeed, that remains true today in England. No British court can overturn a law passed by Parliament. But in the 1760s and 1770s, Americans felt differently.

The citizens of the newly independent states therefore came to believe that the *people* must rule through their legislatures. But they also held that there were higher principles, which the *courts* might enforce. Which would be supreme, democracy or higher judicial authority?

In the years following 1776, the expression of the people's will became dominant: the courts refrained from exercising much power. It was mostly to counteract the excesses of the democratically elected state legislatures that the Constitution was written. The Constitution's objective was to establish a stronger central government. But the role the Supreme Court held in the new central government was unclear.

Most Americans accepted the fact that the Constitution would be superior to the acts of the Congress, the President, and even the courts. But who was to interpret the Constitution? If Congress overstepped its bounds, was it the Supreme Court's duty to keep it in line? If so, who was to keep an eye on the Court to make sure it stayed within its own constitutional boundaries?

After the Constitution was written and its ratification in the states was proceeding, Alexander Hamilton, James Madison, and John Jay wrote a series of articles urging the people of New York to ratify it. These articles were later called the "Federalist Papers," and they rank as probably the greatest political writing America has ever produced.

In the 78th Federalist article Hamilton, the Constitutional Convention delegate from New York, explicitly supported the notion that the Supreme Court could annul an unconstitutional act of Congress. This was a brave statement in an era when all unelected officials were suspect.

The courts, Hamilton wrote, are the least likely to violate the rights of the people. It is the weakest of the three branches of the government, because it has not Congress's power over money, nor the President's power over the armed forces. For the Constitution to survive, Hamilton argued, the Court must be guaranteed complete independence from the other two branches.

Furthermore, he went on, since the Court was so weak, there was no reason to fear its power. Since Congress was particularly strong, the best solution to protect the rights of the people was to have the Court supervise the power of Congress. This way the weakest branch could help the strongest to stay within the bounds set by the Constitution. The duty of the judiciary, Hamilton said, "must be to declare all acts contrary . . . to the constitution void. . . . No legislative act therefore contrary to the constitution can be valid." Hamilton also stated that there was little danger of the Court becoming by itself an unelected "legislature," making new laws simply on its whim.

Soon after the Constitution went into effect, the Supreme Court heard a case brought by a citizen of South Carolina who claimed that the state of Georgia owed him money on a past debt. Georgia stated that it was a "sovereign power," and claimed that it could not be sued unless it gave permission. This it refused to do. In a very strong opinion, the Supreme Court said that Georgia was not a sovereign state and that it therefore had to answer to a suit against it.

But the mood of the country was not yet ready for a

strong judiciary. The reaction to the decision throughout the country was immediate. Everywhere people were saying that the Supreme Court was taking away the basic rights left to the states by the Constitution. Soon afterward, the Eleventh Amendment to the Constitution was passed. It forbade the federal courts from hearing cases begun against a state by a citizen of another state. Following this slap, the Supreme Court settled down to a quiet role, but not for very long.

In the year 1803 the Supreme Court finally took the step which guaranteed it the power to review laws passed by Congress. The subject of the case *Marbury v. Madison* was not of major significance, but the decision reached in it made it the most important Supreme Court case in American history. It was decided in the midst of the most bitter political feud ever to occur in this country.

To understand how vital this case is, we must first go back to 1797, the year in which John Adams became President of the United States. John Adams had been George Washington's friend and Vice-President, and after Washington had completed his two terms as President, Adams was elected to take his place. Adams' own Vice-President was another of Washington's friends, Thomas Jefferson. But Jefferson and Adams were actually serious rivals. They had strong differences in personality, in foreign policy, and in philosophy.

Around Adams a political party had formed called the "Federalists." They believed in a strong central (federal) government, in renewed friendship with Great Britain, and in a strong court system. The supporters of Jefferson had formed a rival party, which was known at first as the "Anti-Federalist" party, but later became known as the "Democrat-Republican," the "Jeffersonian Republican," or simply the "Jeffersonian" party. The Jeffersonians believed that the states should retain more power than the federal government; they championed the cause of revolutionary France; and they feared that the courts would become undemocratic.

Britain and France were at war, and when the United States signed a trading agreement with Britain, the French took it to mean that the Americans were their enemies too.

Relations between the United States and France worsened. Soon the French began seizing American merchant ships on the high seas. Popular feeling against France and its supporters, the Jeffersonians, swept the nation. The Federalist-controlled Congress passed the Alien and Sedition Acts, designed to put in jail any Jeffersonian who criticized the policy against France. This act was enthusiastically enforced by the Federalist judges, earning them the hatred of the Jeffersonian party.

By 1800, the mood of the country had swung the other way, and in the Presidential election Thomas Jefferson defeated John Adams, bringing in with him a Jeffersonian Congress as well.

In those days the new President did not take office until March. In the time left him as President, Adams appointed a number of new Federalist judges. These positions became known as the "midnight appointments," for Adams had to stay up late during the rush of his last days in office in order to complete the appointment papers.

Besides these judges, Adams had the opportunity to make an even more important appointment, that of Chief Justice of the Supreme Court. Adams wanted John Jay, the man who had been the very first Chief Justice under Washington, for the post. But Jay declined Adams' offer, saying that he wanted to stay in New York politics.

Secretary of State John Marshall brought the news of Jay's refusal to President Adams. "Who shall I nominate now?" the President asked. Marshall replied that he could not say. "I believe I must nominate you," Adams said at last, looking at his trusted aide. On hearing this, Marshall bowed his acceptance and quietly left the room.

With Marshall as Chief Justice, Jefferson took office as President in March. Everything was in place for the great battle that was to follow between Jefferson and the Federalist judges.

One of the first things President Jefferson did was to have the Sedition Act repealed. Then the Jeffersonians in Congress impeached and convicted Judge John Pinckney, a Federalist judge from New Hampshire. Pinckney, however, was clearly a drunkard and insane, so the political motives behind his removal were obscured.

But then Congress moved against the Supreme Court itself. The House of Representatives impeached Justice Samuel Chase, a highly partisan Federalist judge who had taken great delight in the prosecution of Jeffersonians under the Sedition Act when Adams was President. The feeling was that if Chase was convicted by the Senate, John Marshall would be the next target.

It was in the midst of these bitter reprisals by the Jeffersonians that the *Marbury v. Madison* case came up before the Supreme Court.

During the waning days of the Adams Administration, when the President had been appointing Federalists to the courts thick and fast, Adams had also appointed some justices of the peace in Washington, D.C. These appointments were duly made and the proper seal attached to them, but some did not get delivered before Adams' term expired. It was John Marshall's job as Secretary of State to see to it that the appointments were delivered. Marshall had continued to be Secretary of State those last few weeks even though he was also Chief Justice. Marshall's brother had undertaken the task of delivering the appointments, but had found so many stacked up on the desk that he had only been able to carry off some of them for delivery.

One of the appointments to justice of the peace that had been left behind was James Marbury's. In March 1801, Thomas Jefferson was inaugurated as President, and when he discovered the leftover appointments, he ordered his new Secretary of State, James Madison, not to deliver them. The last thing he wanted was more Federalist judges!

Needless to say, James Marbury was miffed. He felt he had unjustly been denied his appointment, whereas many other Federalists had received theirs. He decided to bring his complaint to the Supreme Court. Normally, one only reaches the Supreme Court by first going to the lower federal or state courts, and then appealing the case up to the Supreme Court for final decision. (This is called the Supreme Court's *appellate* jurisdiction. It means the Court hears cases on appeal.)

But Marbury decided to take his problem directly to the Supreme Court, without waiting for any lower court to decide his case first. He found that one section of the Judiciary Act of 1789 allowed a person, in certain instances, to skip the appeal process and file the case first with the Supreme Court. (When one goes *first* to the Supreme Court, it is termed using the Court's *original* jurisdiction.) Marbury asked the Court to issue an order compelling Secretary of State James Madison to deliver the commission.

Chief Justice John Marshall was caught in the middle. If he decided in favor of Marbury and ordered Madison to give up the commission, and Madison and Jefferson ignored the order, it would show how weak the Court was in the face of an intransigent executive, and would leave an example for future Presidents to follow. On the other hand, if Marshall gave in to the Jeffersonians and told Marbury he had no right to the commission, it would also show the Court as weak, and would cast doubt on all of Adams' late-term judicial appointments—even Marshall's.

Marshall's solution has been described as the most clever legal ploy in American history. But it was more than that. It was a statement of principles which held the deepest meaning for the American system. First of all, Marshall said, Marbury was entitled to his commission. It was his when the Congress approved the position, when Adams appointed him, and when his commission had been sealed with the official seal of the United States. Marbury owned his commission. It was a denial of his rights for the new Secretary of State to withhold a validly made appointment. Marshall then said that Madison was under a legal obligation to deliver the commission and could not hide behind the powers of the Presidency.

Yet Marshall stopped short of actually ordering Madison to hand over the commission. If Marshall had issued such an order, Jefferson would clearly have ordered Madison to disobey it. Marshall avoided the problem by telling Marbury that even though he deserved the commission, the Supreme Court was without the power to tell Madison to deliver it.

Marshall declared that the section of the Judiciary Act of 1789 which permitted Marbury to bring his case directly to the Supreme Court was itself unconstitutional. He said that the Constitution did not allow Congress to expand the Court's *original* jurisdiction. Therefore, Marbury had come to the wrong place. He would have to start first in a lower court and come up to the Supreme Court only by appeal.

Thus Marshall had established the right of Marbury to his position, but he had avoided confronting the new President in an unequal battle. Most important, he had for the first time in American history declared part of an act of Congress void because it was against the Constitution. By seemingly denying the Court the right to decide Marbury's case, Marshall had actually given the Court vast power. He had established *judicial review*: the right of the Court to review acts of Congress and the President and to declare them invalid if, *in the Court's view*, they were against the Constitution.

Incidentally, Marbury never did try to gain his commission through the lower courts even though Marshall had said that route was open to him. First of all, a justice of the peace commission is held for only a few years. It is not a lifetime appointment, and the period of time Marbury had for the appointment was running out. Secondly, there is evidence that Marbury was a friend or associate of the Marshall family, and he might have been advised to leave well enough alone.

Following *Marbury v. Madison*, Jefferson's campaign against the Federalist judges quickly fell apart. Justice Samuel Chase, although impeached by the House of Representatives, was acquitted in his trial before the Senate. Impeachment as a political weapon against the Court was dead.

The Supreme Court would face many more trials of strength after *Marbury v. Madison*, but its essential position was secure. Its word was final. Impeachment was no check against it, and Constitutional Amendments to change the Court's decisions would be used very rarely.

The debate over judicial review has continued. Many

"WE'RE NUMBER ONE! WE'RE NUMBER ONE!..."

observers believe that the Court's power today has grown far too great. They assert that the Justices are legislating too much and should leave important choices to Congress, the people's representatives. Some fear that democracy is endangered when nine unelected judges can change the country by their own decision. Others hold that the very core of democracy is maintained through the protection of the Court.

CHAPTER THREE

The Division of Powers

Most Americans today look upon the Constitution as a guide for solving nearly all of our social problems. We like to believe that any governmental policy can be found good or bad according to the Constitution. If a federal agency regulates advertisements, someone is bound to call it "unconstitutional." Others think that the Constitution can provide a basis for the day-to-day running of the public school system.

But the fact is, the men who wrote the Constitution in 1787 believed they were creating a very limited document. To them, the Constitution was a charter of narrow powers, not one of broad rights. The framers were concerned with giving enough power to the federal government so that it could rule effectively. But they were equally determined to keep the government from accumulating too much power. Freedom was best protected, they believed, by limiting

"Has anybody seen my copy of the Constitution?"

the power of the Congress and the President to certain specified areas. That way, the government could be kept within proper bounds right from the start.

The concept of limited government was the dominant philosophy behind the Constitution. The early leaders of this country firmly believed that the federal government could make laws in an area only if it found specific permission for it in the Constitution. This became known as the doctrine of *delegated powers.* Whatever powers have not been clearly given to the federal government remain with the people and with the states. If it is not spelled out in the Constitution, then the government may not enter the field.

Let us see how this rule has been applied.

The Powers of Congress. Where does the Congress find the right to pass laws? In the Constitution the Congress is allowed, among other things, to collect taxes, to coin money, to set up post offices, and to support the army. That may seem fairly clear. But can the Congress also print paper money? Can it establish an air force?

We can see that if we limit Congress only to the exact words of the Constitution, it will be powerless to govern this vast country in the complexities of modern life. On the other hand, the Constitution was not written to let Congress do anything it wanted. How do we draw the line?

Chief Justice Marshall gave an answer in *McCulloch v. Maryland* in 1819. In a controversial move, Congress had chartered a national bank. Thomas Jefferson, James Madison, and Andrew Jackson all thought the Congress had no right to set up such a bank (James Madison later changed his mind). These three Presidents pointed out that the

Constitution was silent on the matter. There was, they said, no grant of power to Congress to do such a thing.

Chief Justice Marshall had a different opinion. He reasoned that if the Constitution gave Congress the power to rule in an area, then Congress had the right to choose what it thought was the best way to go about it. The Constitution gave Congress the right to establish a fiscal policy. Therefore, Congress can choose a national bank as a way to accomplish this purpose. In fact, Marshall emphasized, the Constitution itself gives Congress the right "to make all laws which shall be necessary and proper" to the execution of its listed powers. Whether the bank was the best choice Congress could have made was not the Court's business. So long as one could logically find that the bank might help Congress in its fiscal policy, then it was perfectly valid.

The use of the *necessary and proper clause* (Article I, Section 8, of the Constitution) opened the door to broad congressional legislation. A new doctrine developed. Called the doctrine of *implied powers*, it allows Congress to use any means that it can somehow relate to its proper purposes. The Constitution, for instance, permits Congress to "provide for the common defense." For this purpose, Congress may create an air force, build missiles, and use the draft to fill the army.

McCulloch v. Maryland did not solve everything. A serious new problem arose when Congress tried to use one of its constitutional powers to reach into areas outside of what the Constitution permitted. For example, the Constitution gives Congress the right to regulate commerce among the states. Under the necessary and proper clause, Congress may regulate commerce by building new highways, setting a national speed limit, or by establishing rules for ship and barge traffic. These are clearly logical ways to regulate commerce.

Suppose, however, that Congress uses its power over commerce to try to control totally different kinds of activities. This is what Congress started doing in the late 1800s. Among other things, Congress forbade the shipment across state lines of lottery tickets, of goods made by child labor, and even of prostitutes. For a long while the Supreme Court wrestled with this troublesome issue. Sometimes the Court upheld such congressional actions. At other times, it found that Congress had exceeded its constitutional bounds.

In 1937 the Court gave up trying to decide what was a proper *purpose* for Congress in regulating commerce. It decided that economic policy choices should be left up to the Congress. Since then the Court has concentrated on the *means* Congress has chosen to use. Generally speaking, if the means are constitutional, then the purpose will stand.

As a result of the Court's new permissiveness, the interstate commerce clause of the Constitution became one of the most important tools for Congressional legislation. Almost anything now can be regulated by Congress, so long as there is some effect on interstate commerce. A farmer named Filburn found this out to his dismay in 1942.

Under the Agricultural Adjustment Act of 1938, Congress had established limits as to how much wheat farmers could plant. It had hoped to reduce the wheat crop and thus raise prices for the farmer. But there is no constitutional grant to regulate farming. So Congress based the law on its right to control the interstate commerce of farm products.

Filburn was ordered not to plant more than 11.1 acres of wheat. Instead he planted 23 acres, but he used the entire harvest on his farm. Not one bushel crossed state lines. Not one grain entered interstate commerce. When he was fined for exceeding his quota, Filburn refused to pay. He claimed that congressional power should not apply to him, for his wheat had never left his farm.

The Supreme Court held otherwise. It said that if Filburn had not planted the excess acreage, he would have had to buy wheat on the open market for his farm. Therefore, by using his own wheat, Filburn had not bought wheat which normally would have come to him through interstate commerce. Even though Filburn's actions "affected interstate commerce" ever so slightly, that slight effect was enough for Congress's action to be constitutional, for, if all small farmers like Filburn did the same thing, the cumulative effect would seriously affect interstate commerce.

We can see from the Filburn case how wide congressional power has become under the interstate commerce clause. Once the United States developed into a major industrial nation, it became inevitable that Congress's power to regulate commerce would expand. Major social legislation, such as minimum wage laws and anti-discrimination laws regarding restaurants, hotels, and employment, have all been passed under the authority of the commerce clause. These acts have changed the face of our society. Yet Congress still asserts that the regulation is tied to interstate commerce, no matter how local the activity. The formal connection to the constitutional power remains.

The same kind of rule applies to Congress's power to investigate. Many observers feel that this is Congress's most potent weapon. When Senator Sam Ervin led the Watergate investigation, and when Senator Frank Church's subcommittee looked into the illegal activities by the

C.I.A. and the F.B.I., the American people saw what influence such investigations had. The Supreme Court has required that such investigations be directed toward a purpose Congress may constitutionally legislate on. No pure "fishing expeditions" are allowed. But since the Court has given Congress such wide legislative powers over the years, there is now little limitation on what the legislative branch may investigate.

Originally, the Constitution gave only specific law-making power to Congress. Nowadays much has changed. Because of the way in which the Court has interpreted the necessary and proper clause in relation to the commerce clause and other delegated powers, Congress may legislate on most any activity unless the Constitution specifically prohibits it.

The President. Ever since the Supreme Court began its work, it has paid strict attention to the powers of Congress. It has had much less occasion to look into Presidential power. On the whole, the Court has preferred to leave it to Congress, or to the electoral process, to limit Presidential excesses. When the Supreme Court has entered the field, it has usually done so to define which powers were in Congess's hands and which were controlled by the President.

From time to time, for example, Congress has tried to prevent the President from removing Cabinet officers and other executive officers. The legal basis for President Andrew Johnson's impeachment in 1868 was his firing of his Secretary of War in violation of the Tenure of Office Act passed by Congress. Johnson was acquitted in the Senate. At that time the Supreme Court did not have a chance to decide whether Congress could constitutionally restrict the

President in such a fashion. But much later, in *Myers v. U.S.* (1926), the Court did have occasion to face the issue. Then it held that the President has the constitutional power to be free in removing officials in the executive branch. There was no constitutional argument against President Richard M. Nixon's firing of Watergate prosecutor Archibald Cox in 1973, for example. Congress may, however, limit the President's power to remove members of the regulatory agencies, such as the Interstate Commerce Commission (I.C.C.) or the Federal Communications Commission (F.C.C.), for these agencies are theoretically "arms of Congress" and not part of the executive branch.

In recent years the Court has often favored the Congress when it has battled with the President. During the Korean War, President Harry S. Truman ordered his Secretary of Commerce to take possession of the country's steel mills. There had been a strike and the President claimed that the war emergency gave him the right to take over the factories and force the workers back to their jobs. But the Court ordered President Truman to hand back the properties to their owners. Earlier, Congress had specifically rejected giving the President such powers. In the light of that earlier decision, the Court felt obliged to cancel the President's actions.

More recently, President Nixon refused to spend money that Congress had appropriated for specific programs. Although the Supreme Court has not yet squarely faced the issue of "impoundment," as it is called, the lower federal courts have generally found Presidential acts such as these improper.

The Supreme Court has given a broad interpretation to the President's war-making powers. Although the Constitution states that Congress has the right to *declare* war, the

Court has never limited the President's right to *make* war. In the earlier case of *United States v. Curtiss-Wright Export Corp.*, the Court suggested that the President has foreign policy powers going beyond those granted by the Constitution. The Justices asserted that the President is the representative of the United States in the community of nations. In that role, the President has unlimited powers to negotiate for the country and to make commitments. Any limitation on the President must either be spelled out in the Constitution or in laws which Congress may pass. More recently, the Court has begun fastening certain constitutional restrictions on the President's exercise of his power over foreign relations. On the whole, however, the Court has been wary of becoming involved in international affairs.

Although the Court has been hesitant about interfering with the President, Congress has begun moving dramatically into the foreign policy field. In 1973 Congress passed the War Powers Resolution over President Nixon's veto. For the first time in American history, the President's general right to send American troops into battle has been regulated by a general law on the subject. The law declares that the President may order soldiers into armed combat for only sixty days, unless Congress gives permission for a longer period. President Nixon objected strenuously to the new law. He argued that it infringed on the President's constitutional and inherent war-making powers. President Gerald Ford, on the other hand, followed its requirements when he ordered the Marines into Cambodia to rescue the crew of the ship *Mayaguez*, which had been seized on the high seas.

In foreign policy battles, the Supreme Court still prefers to stand aloof. It has not had the chance to test the validity of the War Powers Resolution, and though it has had many opportunities, it avoided deciding whether the Vietnam War was constitutional or not.

There was another confrontation between the Congress and the President, which the Supreme Court wanted to avoid. When the Watergate scandal exploded and Congress began moving toward the impeachment of President Nixon, the Court feared it would be caught in the middle. However, it successfully dodged the hottest issue of them all: what are the constitutional grounds for impeachment?

On February 6, 1974, the crisis surrounding President Nixon had become so intense that the House of Representatives authorized its Judiciary Committee to investigate whether the President should be impeached. During its inquiries, the Judiciary Committee grappled with the problem of what was the proper basis for impeachment. The grounds stated in the Constitution are "Treason, Bribery, or other High Crimes or Misdemeanors." James St. Clair, President Nixon's lawyer, argued that only offenses serious enough to result in jail terms would qualify as grounds. In effect, President Nixon's view was that impeachment was a substitute for a criminal indictment, for he also held that a President could not be tried by a regular court during his term of office.

The counsel for the Judiciary Committee, John Doar, had a different opinion. He believed that the President could be impeached if he *abused the powers* of his office. The grounds listed in the Constitution, Doar held, were only examples of what would constitute Presidential abuse of power.

A third view had been stated by Gerald Ford when he was still a Congressman. During an attempt to have Supreme Court Justice William O. Douglas impeached, Ford said bluntly, "An impeachable offense is whatever a majority of the House of Representatives considers it to be."

The House Judiciary Committee accepted both St. Clair's and Doar's definitions. In voting to recommend impeachment, the committee listed a number of articles of impeachment. The first accused President Nixon of obstructing justice in covering up the Watergate scandal, a clear criminal offense. The second article asserted that the President had abused the powers of his office by using the F.B.I., the C.I.A., and the Secret Service in "disregard of the constitutional rights of citizens." A third article recommended impeachment because the President had refused the Committee's demands for tapes of private White House conversations.

The articles of impeachment were never voted on by the full House of Representatives, nor did President Nixon face trial before the Senate. He resigned before that could take place. But suppose the President had been tried and impeached? Could he have gone to the Supreme Court claiming that the grounds were improper and unconstitutional? Most observers do not think so. The general view is that the sole power of impeachment lies with the House of Representatives and the sole power of conviction with the Senate. There are some areas of constitutional law that are outside the Court's control. Impeachment is probably one of them.

Although the Court did not decide the issue of impeachment, it had entered the fray earlier at a critical point. In his investigation of John Mitchell and the other Watergate defendants, Special Prosecutor Leon Jaworski had asked the federal district court to *subpoena* Nixon's tapes and documents. (A subpoena is an order from a court demanding the production of witnesses or documents.) The President had asked the district court to *quash*, or cancel, the subpoena. When the district judge refused, the case was quickly appealed to the Supreme Court.

The President asserted that the Constitution gave him the right of secrecy in his own department. The Court, he said, could not enter into the internal workings of the executive branch without violating the separation of powers required by the Constitution. Theoretically the President has the right to keep certain documents secret from Congress and the courts by a principle called *executive privilege*.

In the case of *United States v. Nixon* (1974), the Supreme Court unanimously agreed that there may be occasions for executive privilege, especially if military or diplomatic secrets are involved. But in this instance the Court found that the needs of the courts in their criminal investigations ought to come first. If the required documents were not available for scrutiny, the essential powers of the judicial branch would be compromised. The Supreme Court ordered President Nixon to produce the tapes. It was these tapes that proved how deep was the President's complicity in the Watergate affair and forced his resignation.

The Court. As might be expected, the Supreme Court has shown much favoritism in its own claims to constitutional authority. We have already seen how judicial review was established in *Marbury v. Madison.* In contests with Congress and the President, the Court has not been shy of late in asserting its own power.

For one thing, it gave itself subpoena power over Presidential documents in *United States v. Nixon.* In addition to establishing its right to intervene in the internal workings

DOWN TO SIZE

of the executive department, the Supreme Court has also reviewed the way in which Congress regulates itself.

In 1966 Adam Clayton Powell was reelected to the House of Representatives. Although a popular political leader, Powell was at that time under a cloud: he was being investigated for having used government expense account funds for his own personal requirements. In March of 1967 the House of Representatives found his conduct unethical. By a vote of 307 to 116, the House voted to exclude Powell from taking his seat in Congress.

The House of Representatives based its right to exclude Powell on Article I, Section 5, of the Constitution. Part of this section reads: "Each House shall be the Judge of the . . . Qualifications of its own Members. . . . Each House may . . . with the Concurrence of two-thirds, expel a Member."

Powell asked the federal courts to issue an injunction which would assure him of his seat in Congress. By tradition, each branch of government is thought to be master of its own house, in control of its own internal procedures. But in this case, the Supreme Court concluded that the House of Representatives had wrongly *excluded* Powell. It left open the question of whether Congress has an absolute right to *expel* one of its members.

The decisions in the *Nixon* and *Powell* cases demonstrate that the Court will not avoid decisions that affect the internal workings of the other two branches. Yet the courts carefully guard their own powers. Recently, for example, a number of grand juries have been demanding testimony from newspaper reporters. In several cases reporters have been asked to reveal the sources of some of their news stories. If a reporter failed to divulge this information, he was frequently cited for *contempt* by the judge and sent to jail. In 1972 a number of these cases came together before the Supreme Court.

In a 5 to 4 decision, the Court declared that reporters must testify before grand juries concerning their confidential sources. The dissenters believed that the right of a free press depended on the reporters being able to keep the identity of their informants secret. But the majority held that reporters, like all citizens, have a duty to testify regarding criminal activities they have knowledge of.

The Supreme Court has also supported the judicial process in other instances. It has upheld the right of a judge to order a disruptive defendant to be bound, gagged, or removed from the courtroom. However, the Court has said that in the case of a lawyer being cited for contempt, the hearing on the contempt citation must either be held immediately or, if put off, held before a different judge.

Similarly, the Justices have indicated less sympathy for public demonstrations held in or near courthouses than ones held in other public places. Take the landmark case of *Cox v. Louisiana*, for example. In late 1961 a Congregational minister, B. Elton Cox, led a protest march of 2,000 students in Baton Rouge, Louisiana. The group marched to the courthouse in order to demonstrate against the arrest of other student marchers the day before.

During the demonstration there were a few very minor disturbances, and Reverend Cox was arrested. He was convicted for violating three laws: disturbing the peace, obstructing public passages, and picketing before a courthouse. Hearing the case on appeal, the Supreme Court had little difficulty in dismissing the first two convictions. It found that in fact Cox and the students had not disturbed the peace, and that the police had applied the law against obstructing public passages in a discriminatory way.

THE GOOSE THAT LAID THE GOLDEN EGG

The Court, however, was less sure of the injustice of the conviction for picketing near a courthouse. The majority believed such a law was valid and even necessary to keep the courts free from the pressures of the mob. But since most of the Justices thought the record showed that the police had given permission for the picketing anyway, Cox was acquitted. Three dissenters, led by Justice Hugo Black, would have upheld Cox's conviction on this count.

The Supreme Court generally puts up a solid front when violence or blunt obstructionism is used against orders issued by lower federal courts. Particularly in cases where desegregation orders in the South were greeted by violence, the Supreme Court has backed up the lower federal judges.

Finally, judges at all levels enjoy immunity from suit in all their official actions. A mother in Indiana had requested a state judge there to order that her 15-year-old daughter be sterilized. The mother claimed that the girl was slightly retarded. The judge granted the order, even though there was no one to represent the interests of the daughter. When she was taken to the hospital to be sterilized, the girl was told only that she was to have her appendix removed.

Two years later the girl was married, and when she failed to become pregnant, she discovered that her "appendectomy" had really been a sterilization. She and her husband sued a number of the parties involved, including the state judge. The judge said that he was immune from suit. Even though he may have abridged the girl's constitutional rights, he was protected in his judicial actions. The Supreme Court of the United States agreed in a 5 to 3 decision. The only way a judge can be sued, the Court declared, is when he acts clearly outside of his proper jurisdiction. But if the judge has jurisdiction, then his judicial

"ALL RISE!"

actions are immune from suit even if what he did was done in error or maliciously.

In contests with other branches of government, or with the states, and particularly where violence is part of the resistance, the Supreme Court can be expected to protect its own.

The States. The founding fathers believed that the best way to protect freedom was to prevent a concentration of power in the national government. We saw how the powers of the government were divided among the three branches. And we also know that these powers are limited to only those that the Constitution expressly delegates to the national government.

But we must also look at a factor at least as important: the residual power of the states. The founding fathers fully expected that the states would remain the dominant centers of power within the nation. James Madison argued that with so many states in the union, the chances for one oppressive faction to take control everywhere was impossible. He thought this one of the great protections for the people. Even today, the states retain what is called the "police power." This power does not refer directly to the men and women in blue uniforms who patrol the city streets. Rather, it refers to the *inherent* power of a state to legislate on the health, welfare, and morals of the people who live inside the state. For example, the laws on job safety, traffic control, drugs, and education are written mostly by the states, not by the federal government.

If we search through the Constitution, we find no mention of police power. The Constitution does not give the states this power. The states already had it before the Constitution was written. They had it in 1776 when independence was declared, and they kept it after the Constitution went into effect.

Certain powers were given up to the federal government by the people of the states when they ratified the Constitution. The Constitution lists the areas into which the states are forbidden to enter. For example, there are certain flat prohibitions applied to the states. They may not sign treaties with foreign countries or coin money or make tariffs or create titles of nobility such as Duke or Earl. The states also are forbidden to pass *ex post facto* laws—that is to say, laws which make a past action a crime even though it was committed before the law was passed. The Constitution, as interpreted by the Supreme Court, requires that state laws shall not infringe on some of the protections of the Bill of Rights. We shall look closely at these problems later on.

One of the most troublesome issues which has faced the Court has been that of defining which powers belong to the federal government and which remain with the states. Unfortunately, sometimes the Constitution is not clear about where the powers lie. We know that some powers, such as making war or printing money, are lodged exclusively with the federal government. The real problem comes where both the states and the federal government have powers in the same areas. This is called *concurrent jurisdiction*. And if there is a conflict, which law is superior—the states' or Congress's?

In almost all instances where Congress has the power to legislate, the states must give way. The Constitution itself declares that the "Laws of the United States . . . shall be the supreme Law of the Land." So long as Congress exercises its power constitutionally, contrary state laws are invalid. We saw, for example, how the Commerce Clause gives Congress the right to control activities even inside the state (intrastate activities) if they affect commerce outside the state. Thus, the federal government has set minimum wages for workers whose products in some way use or will affect goods in interstate commerce.

But can the states do the same thing? Can they legislate on an internal matter even though it affects subjects which are supposed to be left to the federal government?

Let us recall the case of *McCulloch v. Maryland*. In that case John Marshall declared that the Congress could charter a national bank under the necessary and proper clause. But there was a second issue in that case. Maryland had levied a tax on the Baltimore branch of the Bank of the United States. The Bank refused to pay. Maryland argued that it had the right to tax business within its own state. Even if the Bank of the United States had a right to exist, why could not Maryland tax the Baltimore branch of the bank? Why should this bank be free from taxes simply because it was owned by the federal government? John Marshall found this argument unconvincing. In his famous phrase, "the power to tax involves the power to destroy," he declared that the state cannot use its power over internal matters to cripple a legitimate federal activity. The Constitution requires that in case of a conflict, federal rights dominate. Therefore, even in instances where the state has a legitimate right, it must give way if it comes in conflict with a right of the federal government.

Take, for example, the case of *Bibb v. Navajo Freight Lines, Inc.* During the 1950s, the state of Illinois enacted a law requiring trucks to use a rear mudguard which was curved. Straight mudguards became illegal in that state. However, in at least forty-five of the other states, the straight mudguard was legal. In fact, the state of Arkansas

required it. Navajo Freight Lines challenged the Illinois law
in federal court, and the Supreme Court agreed with the
trucking company. The Court said that it was not deciding
whether straight mudguards were better or worse than the
curved type. That was up to the states to determine. But
where one state required a curved mudguard, forcing all
trucks to change equipment when they crossed into the
state, it was an "unreasonable burden" on interstate commerce. Such laws are invalid. Congressional power over
interstate commerce cannot be crippled by state laws.

The Supreme Court will allow an internal state law to
stand, even if it affects interstate commerce, provided its
out-of-state effects are only "incidental" and they are not
an unreasonable burden on interstate commerce. On the
other hand, a state is usually denied the right to regulate
its internal affairs if Congress has already moved into
the field under its constitutional powers. States may not,
for instance, set railroad rates for trains operating wholly
within their borders, because Congress has put the entire
subject under the control of the Interstate Commerce
Commission.

There are also situations in which Congress specifically
allows the states to pass laws in a federal area. In these situations the Court will permit the states to act. A year after
the Illinois mudguard statute was struck down, a Detroit
air pollution ordinance came before the Court. Detroit had
applied strict pollution control laws to ships entering its
harbors. These controls were far more extensive than those
in other cities or in other states. Consequently, to use Detroit's harbors, ships which traveled in interstate commerce
were forced to undertake costly alterations to their boilers.

One shipping company claimed that the law was an unreasonable burden on interstate commerce. The company

undoubtedly felt that Detroit's pollution law interfered with commerce far more than did the Illinois mudguard statute. But the Supreme Court did not agree. The Justices gave special consideration to the fact that the Congress had at that time openly left pollution regulation to the states.

Nonetheless, with the expansion of the commerce power of Congress, many observers have come to the conclusion that there is almost no constitutionally protected area of exclusive state power any longer. States can legislate, the argument goes, only because Congress has chosen not to enter certain fields fully.

Today, there are few areas of state concern which remain constitutionally protected from congressional or judicial revision. It used to be accepted that the states were able to draw the lines of their election districts as they saw fit. A state could, if it wished, form its senate districts along county lines and its house of representative districts according to population. Sometimes, this resulted in one sparsely populated district having the same representation as districts holding many more voters. In 1946 the Supreme Court called this a "political" issue—that is, a question to be decided not by judges but by the voters and their representatives. Even in drawing their congressional districts, the states could be corrected only by the Congress, not by the Court.

During the 1960s, however, the Supreme Court abruptly changed its mind. In *Wesberry v. Sanders* (1964) and *Reynolds v. Sims* (1964), it ruled that congressional and state election districts had to contain the same numbers of people. The Constitution, the Court said, required this result. It was no longer a political question. The states did not have constitutional immunity in this field.

In a number of decisions that followed, the Supreme Court ordered that the states must draw their election districts so that each one would hold approximately the same amount of people. This includes districts for members of Congress, state representatives, state senators, and even many local offices. However, the Court has held that state legislative districts could be drawn less strictly than congressional districts. Each congressional district within a state must have an equal number of people—at least as close as is practical. But state legislative districts can be based on the number of registered voters only. In addition, the Court has recently tolerated a wider variation in numbers of voters between state districts than between congressional districts. Nonetheless, what used to be thought of as an area of exclusive state concern is now strictly regulated by the Court.

Do these decisions mean that the states can no longer act independently? Many people had begun to think so. But in 1976 the Supreme Court itself contradicted this view in the closely divided case of *National League of Cities v. Usery*.

Two years before, in 1974, Congress had passed a statute expanding the coverage of its minimum-wage regulations. The new law covered people who were working for the states and cities. Taking the issue to the United States District Court in the District of Columbia, the National League of Cities sought to have the law's requirements blocked. When the district court dismissed the complaint, the cities lodged their appeal with the Supreme Court.

In a new feeling of concern for the states, the Court cut down the congressional action. The decision held that the effect of the law was to impinge upon the fundamental constitutional protections afforded the states. The Tenth

Amendment reserves to the states all powers not delegated to the federal government, and the Court held that Congress violated the Tenth Amendment when it dictated to the states how to treat the state's own employees. It was the first such action by the Court in many years. Speaking for the five-man majority, Justice William Rehnquist said that the Court must recognize "the essential role of the states in our federal system of government." Such an incursion by Congress may curtail the state's essential political functions, he wrote. That area is reserved for the states alone, and Congress may not enter.

Although the decision in the *Usery* case shows a renewed respect for the constitutional autonomy of the states, the states have never really lost their autonomy in certain recognized areas of independence. Congress may not levy a tax which places a substantial burden on a state's essential functions, for example. The Constitution also protects the states from being divided up or joined with other states without their consent. In addition, no state can be denied its complement of two United States senators in Washington.

Finally, the Supreme Court does defer to state court decisions which interpret state law. The high Court will only hear federal questions on appeal from state courts. Frequently, the appealing party loses in the state court on the basis of both state law and federal law. In such cases, the Supreme Court will not even hear the federal issue on appeal, for the appellant would lose his case anyway on the basis of state law. This is called the doctrine of *independent state grounds*.

In addition, the Court will sometimes refuse to hear a valid federal claim—one which would change the result in a case—if the losing party failed to observe proper state judicial procedures in asserting his claim. For example, claims must be made within the time limits that state law requires. If the losing party thinks of a federal issue too late under state law, the Supreme Court will usually reject his appeal.

In the last few decades, both the real power and the constitutional rights of the federal government have vastly increased. But the practical significance of the federal system remains. The states are still a center of major legislative policies. In addition, they retain certain core constitutional protections, to which the Court has shown more sensitivity of late.

CHAPTER FOUR

The Rights of the Individual

When the framers of the Constitution finished their work, they submitted the document to the people of the states for ratification. During the debates in the state ratifying conventions, time and again delegates objected to the absence of many specific guarantees of personal liberty in the Constitution. The framers were a bit taken aback by these charges, for they did not believe that there was a need for an additional list of guarantees. Congress, they said, only possesses the powers which are in the Constitution. Since the Constitution does not give Congress any power to regulate the press, for example, Congress simply had no right to legislate on the matter.

But the state conventions were not convinced. Many of the delegates felt that the new central government would have too much power over the states and the people. They wanted more safeguards.

As a result, the Constitution was ratified—but only on the condition that amendments would be added to guard certain rights. The bargain was kept. As soon as the first Congress was called to order in 1789, it set to work drawing up a Bill of Rights—the first ten amendments to the Constitution. Today these amendments are considered the cornerstone of the rights of a free people.

The most important guarantees in the Bill of Rights are:

In the First Amendment:	No state religion. Freedom of religion. Freedom of speech. Freedom of the press. The right of assembly.
In the Second Amendment:	The limited right to bear arms.
In the Third Amendment:	Freedom from having soldiers quartered in one's house.
In the Fourth Amendment:	Freedom from unreasonable searches and seizures. The requirement of a search warrant.
In the Fifth Amendment:	The requirement of indictment by grand jury. Freedom from being tried twice for the same crime. Freedom from self-incrimination. Limited protection from having one's property confiscated. Protection of one's life, liberty, and property, under due process of law.

In the Sixth Amendment:	The right to a speedy and public trial. The right to a jury trial. The right to know what one is charged with. The right to cross-examine witnesses. The right to have an attorney.
In the Seventh Amendment:	The right in certain civil cases to have a jury trial.
In the Eighth Amendment:	Protection against cruel and unusual punishments.
In the Ninth Amendment:	The recognition that the people have other rights besides those that are listed in the Constitution.
In the Tenth Amendment:	The recognition that powers not listed in the Constitution are retained by the states or by the people.

It was clear from the beginning that the Bill of Rights applied only to the federal government. The amendments held the feared central government in check. The states were left free to do as they saw fit. In a letter to Abigail Adams, Thomas Jefferson wrote "While we deny that Congress have a right to control the freedom of press, we have ever asserted the right of the states, and their exclusive right to do so."

Of course, most of the states had guarantees of personal freedom in their own state constitutions. Nevertheless, as Chief Justice Marshall said in the case of *Barron v. Baltimore* (1833), the Bill of Rights in the federal Constitution "must be understood as restraining the power to the general government, not as applicable to the states."

The neat division between restrictions on the federal government and freedom of action for the states was dramatically changed by the Thirteenth, Fourteenth, and Fifteenth amendments to the Constitution, which came into being shortly after the Civil War. The purpose of all three of the amendments was to guarantee full citizenship rights to the freed slaves. The Thirteenth Amendment forbade slavery, and the Fifteenth gave the blacks the right to vote. But the most important of the post-Civil War amendments was the Fourteenth, which was written to assure the freed black slaves that they would have the same fundamental legal rights as did white people.

The key section of the Fourteenth Amendment reads as follows:

> No state shall make or enforce any law which shall abridge the privileges or immunities of citizens of the United States, nor shall deprive any person of life, liberty or property, without due process of law, nor deny to any person within its jurisdiction the equal protection of the laws.

The question was: What kinds of protection did these new guarantees give the people against arbitrary state action? Within five years of the ratification of the Fourteenth Amendment, a claim was made that this amendment took all of the Bill of Rights and applied the same protections now against the state governments. This later became known as the doctrine of *incorporation*. (At first, some people looked to the *privileges and immunities clause* of the Fourteenth Amendment as the "carrier" of the freedoms in the Bill of Rights. Later, however, most found the *due process clause* as the best route.)

When the Supreme Court first looked at the issue in 1873 in the *Slaughterhouse Cases,* a majority of five rejected the idea that the Fourteenth Amendment was a shorthand version of the Bill of Rights. The minority was not discouraged. These Justices insisted that the only way to prevent a deprivation of rights by the states was to make sure that all of the guarantees in the first ten amendments (or at least the first eight amendments) applied against the states as well as against the federal government.

The issue did not die. For almost a century after the *Slaughterhouse Cases,* the Supreme Court continued to debate whether the due process clause of the Fourteenth Amendment had anything to do with the Bill of Rights. One group of Justices, led by Justice Hugo Black, insisted that the due process clause was meant to be a carbon copy of the Bill of Rights. Whatever the first eight amendments said, the Fourteenth Amendment said. Justice Black's view became known as the theory of *total incorporation.* As he said to the Court, "I would follow what I believe was the original purpose of the Fourteenth Amendment—to extend to all the people of the nation the complete protection of the Bill of Rights."

Opposed to Justice Black's view were the opinions of Justice Felix Frankfurter. Frankfurter asked a simple question: If the framers of the Fourteenth Amendment meant it to incorporate the Bill of Rights, why did they not say so directly, instead of using a vague phrase such as "due process of law"? To Frankfurter, the due process clause of the Fourteenth Amendment was completely independent of the Bill of Rights. The restrictions on the states created by the Fourteenth Amendment were not necessarily the same restrictions on the federal government which were written into the Bill of Rights. The Fourteenth Amendment stood by itself, Frankfurter said. It had an *independent potency.*

In turn, many people asked Frankfurter, if the due process clause of the Fourteenth Amendment is different from the Bill of Rights, what then does "due process of law" mean? Here, Frankfurter gave a traditional answer. Due process of law means basic fairness at trial. (This is usually termed *procedural due process.*) States must make sure that their courts operate under basic rules of fairness. For example, a defendant must be told, or "given notice," that there is a suit against him, so that he can defend himself in court. A judge cannot preside over a case in which he has a direct personal interest as to who wins or loses. It was in these kinds of areas that the Fourteenth Amendment protected against state procedural violations, and the Supreme Court would make sure that the amendment was enforced. Sometimes, of course, a right protected by the Fourteenth Amendment was also protected by the Bill of Rights. For example, the Sixth Amendment requires that in federal cases the accused shall "be informed of the nature and cause of the accusation." This is the same requirement of "notice" which the Fourteenth Amendment requires in state trials. But, Frankfurter would say, the due process clause of the Fourteenth Amendment would compel fair notice by the states even if the Sixth Amendment did not require it of the federal government. The two amendments are independent of one another.

Yet Frankfurter had a serious problem with this point of view. What rights of fair procedure does the due process clause require? At least there is a relatively clear list in the Bill of Rights. The Fourteenth Amendment has no such list—only the words "due process of law." For some years, even before Frankfurter was appointed to the Court, the Justices had been struggling to find some kind of formula to determine what rights the due process clause protected and what rights it did not. The key case in the search was *Palko v. Connecticut,* decided in 1937. Palko had been charged with first-degree murder, but the jury returned a verdict of guilty of murder in the second degree. The prosecution, representing the state of Connecticut, appealed and asked for a new trial. It won the appeal, and Palko went on trial again for first-degree murder. This time he was convicted of the charge and was sentenced to be executed. He appealed his case to the Supreme Court.

Without a doubt, if the federal government had tried Palko twice, the second trial would have been disallowed. The Fifth Amendment clearly forbids "double jeopardy." But does the due process clause of the Fourteenth Amendment forbid it also? Palko argued that he deserved the same protection in a state court as he would have in a federal court. The Court was deeply divided on the issue. Writing for the majority, Justice Benjamin Cardozo said that the Fourteenth Amendment will "absorb" only those rights which were "of the very essence of a scheme of ordered liberty." Was the protection against double jeopardy necessary to a scheme of ordered liberty? Could a "fair and enlightened system of justice" operate when someone is tried a second time as a result of the prosecution's successfully appealing the first result? Justice Cardozo thought that a prohibition against double jeopardy was not really basic to a free society. Therefore, the second conviction of Palko would stand. It did not violate the due process clause of the Fourteenth Amendment.

For the next twenty-five years this independent view of

the due process clause, mainly championed by Justice Frankfurter, was dominant in the Court. Justice Black continued to call for the complete incorporation of the Bill of Rights into the due process clause, but he was never able to convince a majority of the Court. Nevertheless, a third view of the due process clause arose, which eventually carried the day. Some Justices looked at the Palko decision not as supporting an independent view of the Fourteenth Amendment, but rather as standing for the idea that the Fourteenth Amendment did in fact take some of the protections of the Bill of Rights and apply them against the states. However, unlike Justice Black, who wanted all of the Bill of Rights incorporated, these Justices insisted that only some should be incorporated into the Fourteenth Amendment. This soon became known as the theory of *selective incorporation*. Well, which ones, Frankfurter and Black both asked, should be selected and which ones should be left out?

Here the selective incorporationists used the Palko formula of Justice Cardozo. Those parts of the Bill of Rights "necessary to a scheme of ordered liberty" would be placed in the Fourteenth Amendment. Those parts not essential to liberty would be left out. Thus, three views concerning the Fourteenth Amendment, all in conflict with each other, arose: (1) total incorporation of the Bill of Rights, (2) selective incorporation of the Bill of Rights, and (3) a view that the Fourteenth Amendment was independent of the Bill of Rights.

By the 1960s, under the Warren Court, the selective incorporationists finally gained a clear majority. By that time, all of the First Amendment guarantees had already been made part of the due process clause. The Court had also required states to provide defendants with a lawyer if the charge could result in a death sentence. States were also prohibited from using certain kinds of illegally seized evidence at trial. But, during the 1960s, nearly all the rest of the guarantees of the Bill of Rights were incorporated: (1) the right to have an attorney in all serious criminal cases; (2) the exclusion at trial of all evidence which the police had seized illegally; (3) the right against self-incrimination; (4) the right to a speedy, public trial; (5) the right to cross-examine witnesses; (6) the right to subpoena witnesses (that is, to order them to appear at trial); (7) the right to a jury trial; (8) the prohibition of double jeopardy (in *Benton v. Maryland,* 1969, overruling *Palko v. Connecticut*); (9) the requirement that conviction must be beyond a reasonable doubt. In fact, by the end of the 1960s, all the Bill of Rights had been selectively incorporated into the due process clause of the Fourteenth Amendment except for: (1) the requirement that indictment (that is, the official criminal charges against a person) be by grand jury and (2) the right of defendants to a jury trial in ordinary civil (non-criminal) cases. All of the other protections afforded by the Bill of Rights were now applied to state action.

The Court today, however, is still troubled by the issue of incorporation. Chief Justice Warren Burger continues to criticize the rule which excludes using illegally seized evidence in state trials. Another ongoing problem is the issue of the right to a jury trial. That right is protected in federal trials by the Sixth Amendment, and by incorporation, is also protected in state trials by the Fourteenth Amendment. So far, it would seem to be a simple issue. But one state did not see it that way.

Florida is required to grant defendants a jury trial in criminal cases. The only problem is that Florida requires a six-person jury (except in death penalty cases), not a twelve-person jury as is required in federal trials. But the Sixth Amendment does not state how large the jury must be. It only says, "In all criminal prosecutions, the accused shall enjoy the right to a speedy and public trial, by an impartial jury. . . ." Is the twelve-person jury really part of the Sixth Amendment, even though it does not say so directly?

Justice John Marshall Harlan, who followed Justice Frankfurter's ideas on the Fourteenth Amendment, had no trouble with the issue. For him, the requirements of the Sixth Amendment were different from the requirements of the Fourteenth Amendment. The history of the Sixth Amendment, Justice Harlan held, showed federal juries must have twelve persons. The Fourteenth Amendment, on the other hand, required a jury only as a rule of fairness at trial, and six persons would be enough to obtain a fair cross section of the community. But the other Justices did not agree with Justice Harlan. They believed that the Sixth and Fourteenth amendments were the same in this regard, and the majority held that a six-person jury was all that was constitutionally necessary. The federal twelve-person jury was merely a rule of the Court which could be changed without violating the Constitution. Justice Thurgood Marshall dissented. He also thought the Sixth and Fourteenth amendments meant the same thing, only he believed both necessitated twelve-person juries as a constitutional requirement.

This Florida case, called *Williams v. Florida* (1970), illustrated one of the continuing problems of incorporation. Justices Frankfurter and Harlan would have applied the Bill of Rights strictly to the federal government, but would have allowed the states a little more leeway to experiment under the due process clause of the Fourteenth Amendment. Under total incorporation, on the other hand, the requirements are the same for both the state governments and the federal government. This led Justice Harlan to fear that the final result will not be *more* protection for the people in *state* courts, but ultimately *less* protection for them in *federal* courts.

There is some logic in Justice Harlan's point of view. The issue of the right to a jury trial led to a bizarre result in the case of *Apodaca v. Oregon* (1972). In that case, Oregon required a vote of only ten of the twelve jurors for conviction in a criminal case not involving the death penalty. When the Supreme Court reviewed this procedure, eight Justices said they thought the Sixth and Fourteenth Amendments had an identical requirement, but they differed on what that requirement was. Four Justices believed that the incorporated Sixth Amendment compelled unanimous jury verdicts, while the other four said that non-unanimous jury verdicts were acceptable in both state and federal courts. Only Justice Lewis Powell, following Justice Harlan's philosophy, claimed there was a difference. The Sixth Amendment, he said, made unanimous jury verdicts mandatory in federal trials, but the due process clause of the Fourteenth Amendment allowed non-unanimous verdicts in state trials. Thus Powell voted with the four Justices who felt non-unanimous verdicts were acceptable. Because of Justice Powell's vote, Oregon and other states may now use less than a unanimous vote for conviction. However, it is not likely that Justice Powell's distinction between the different requirements of the Sixth and Fourteenth amendments will hold up over time. Most of the Court is now firmly of the opinion that the due process clause of the Fourteenth Amendment and nearly all of the Bill of

Rights impose identical rules on the states and the federal government. As a matter of fact, in *Colgreve v. Battin* (1973), the Supreme Court decided that a federal district court could require a six-person jury in civil cases.

GUARANTEES OF THE BILL OF RIGHTS

Let us now turn to those freedoms which are protected by the Bill of Rights, and through incorporation, by the Fourteenth Amendment as well.

The First Amendment may indeed be the most important, for the very basis of a democratic society lies in the ability of a people to communicate their beliefs and opinions. For this reason, the Supreme Court tends to be suspicious of a law which in some way restricts freedom of speech or of the press. Many Justices believe that freedoms such as those protected by the First Amendment have a "preferred position" in the Constitution and that restrictive laws can be allowed in only the most exceptional circumstances.

The words of the First Amendment, "Congress shall make no law . . . abridging the freedom of speech, or of the press," are deceptively simple. First of all, through the Fourteenth Amendment, the protection applies to states as well as to Congress. Second, even though the words do not say so, the executive branch is also prohibited from abridging the freedom of speech. Third, what does "abridgement" mean? Is any restriction on speech invalid? The Court has always said that certain abridgements may be allowed in certain cases. Fourth, what is the "freedom" in freedom of speech? Can one say anything to anybody at any time? In Justice Oliver Wendell Holmes' famous phrase, "The most stringent protection of free speech would not protect a man in falsely shouting 'Fire!' in a crowded theatre and causing a panic." Finally, what is speech? Are signs speech? Is a silent protest speech? Indeed, is pornography speech? Let us look at some of the aspects of freedom of speech to see how that right is protected in today's Court.

I. Speech Itself

Under what conditions may Congress or the states punish someone simply for uttering words? Obviously, if someone convinces another to rob a bank, the first person can be prosecuted as an accessory to the bank robbery. The First Amendment does not protect that kind of speech. And if two or more persons merely discuss a jointly held plan to rob a bank and then begin to take the steps to bring their plan to success, they can be prosecuted for conspiracy even before the actual robbery.

What if someone makes a speech proclaiming that democracy is a failure and that only a violent revolution can save the country? Speeches and pamphlets like these first brought the Supreme Court into the field shortly after World War I. In *Schenck v. The United States* (1919), Justice Holmes first put forward his famous test of "clear and present danger." However, for many years, it was unclear what kind of speech brought about a clear and present danger of an illegal act. For a while, even the Court rejected the clear and present danger test in favor of a much looser test which held that any speech tending to bring about some eventual harm could be punished. However, during the 1950s and 1960s, the clear and present danger test resurfaced, and today its meaning is relatively clear. Basically, the state can punish speech itself if the words are a direct incitement to an illegal act. Recent cases also suggest that for speech to be punishable, the illegal act must be likely to happen immediately following the speech and not at some unclear time in the future. On the other hand, if someone is only speaking about a political belief, then the speaker is protected. For example, if a leftist says that the time will come in the United States when the workers will rise up and take over the government by force, then this is a case of belief, not incitement.

II. The Effects of Speech

Suppose an American Nazi is making a speech in a Jewish neighborhood. He calls Jews by foul names, insults their heritage, and praises Hitler as a great man. The crowd which gathers around him is not likely to be very friendly. If they become angry, there is the danger that they can turn violent. Most states have "breach of the peace" statutes which are designed to maintain public order. In a case such as this, could the police arrest the Nazi speaker to prevent a riot? Or should they control the crowd? Notice that in this case, the speaker is not inciting supporters to become violent. Rather it is those who oppose him who are likely to become violent.

The Supreme Court has decided similar cases both ways. On some occasions it has upheld the arrest of the speaker, on others it has found the arrest unconstitutional. The recent trend seems to be, however, that a person's right to speak cannot be limited by the reaction of those who may oppose his ideas. We cannot let the majority veto the right of a minority to speak its mind. However, in circumstances where a riot is imminent, and where the control of the crowd by the police is impossible, the Court has upheld the arrest of a speaker who refused to step down after being asked to do so by the police. Outside of these unusual circumstances, the Court will normally seek to protect the right of the speaker to express unpopular views.

III. Symbolic Speech

Mary Beth Tinker was caught up in the wave of antiwar sentiment during the Vietnam conflict. In 1965, along with other students from her school, she had decided to wear a black arm band in school to protest the war. Two days before she made her protest, the principals of the schools in Des Moines, Iowa, where Mary Beth lived, voted to ban the wearing of arm bands because they feared it would disrupt school activities. In fact, most of the people of Des Moines, including the students, were in favor of the United States involvement in Vietnam. When Mary Beth Tinker and some other students arrived at school wearing arm bands, they were told to take them off. They refused. The principal suspended them from school and sent them home.

In 1968, *Tinker v. Des Moines School District* reached the Supreme Court. Of course a school can restrict disruptive speech, but the first question here was whether wearing arm bands is speech at all. The Court found that this was like "pure speech." It was not conduct. As such, it expressed a particular point of view which could not be suppressed unless, of course, the arm bands prevented classes from proceeding normally (which the Court found not to be the case here) .

The dividing line between actions which are symbolic speech and actions which are conduct is hard to draw. People kill one another sometimes for political reasons.

Clearly, this is not "speech." In one case, a young man who opposed the military draft scrawled an obscenity on the back of his jacket. He was arrested for wearing the jacket in a public building where it would offend those that had to be present for one reason or another. But the Supreme Court declared his arrest invalid. So long as the young man was not trying to incite disobedience to the draft, he was protected in expressing his views as he saw fit.

On the other hand, another man opposed to the draft publicly burned his draft card in violation of a congressional law prohibiting the mutilation of draft cards. Here the Court found that this was not a case of symbolic speech, but one of conduct which Congress had good reason to forbid. Thus far, it is fair to say that the Court has not yet developed standards to tell what is symbolic speech and what is conduct. But it seems reasonable to expect that the Court will limit the idea of symbolic speech to an act which has no importance outside of the idea it is expressing. Wearing a "Vote For Carter" button has no significance outside of the idea it is expressing. But if a partisan Democrat throws a rock through the window of the Republican Party headquarters, then the act has a different significance—destroying property.

Even so, there are cases where it is hard to distinguish symbolic expression from conduct. In the recent case of *Buckley v. Valeo* (1976), the Court suggested that contributing money to a political campaign was a form of expression which deserved some constitutional protection. On the other hand, the Court has many times said that picketing is not symbolic speech. Picketing can be regulated by the state. Even though people are carrying signs with a message, they are really using the public streets, and that is formal conduct which can be regulated.

IV. Regulating Speech

In order to prevent littering, may a city require that someone seek government permission before handing out leaflets? No. In order to keep the streets orderly, may a city require persons who want to parade to get a permit first? Yes. The area of regulating speech is a most difficult one for the Court to come to grips with. In these instances, the city usually does not want to suppress speech, but wants to do something it ordinarily has a right to do. Cities have the right to keep the streets litter free, to keep traffic flowing, and to maintain public order. To distinguish proper laws from improper ones, the Supreme Court has evolved a number of questions it asks in such cases. Here are some of them:

Is the statute clear? An ordinary person must be able to understand what actions are legal and what actions are illegal. If the law is unclear, it is "void for vagueness." This is true of any law, whether it deals with free speech or some other subject.

Is the statute overbroad? Sometimes a statute is clear enough, but the acts it prohibits unnecessarily include protected rights such as free speech. For example, the law which limits leaflets and other publications in order to keep the streets clean is overbroad. It restricts free speech when there are more narrow means available. The city could simply punish those who litter.

Is the statute invalid as applied? Sometimes the statute is clear and not overbroad. But the police may apply it improperly. A valid statute to prevent breaches of the peace does not allow the police to use that law to suppress public speakers whom they do not like.

Does the law regulate the manner of speaking or the

content of the speech? This is the key question. The Court will always scrutinize the law to make sure it reasonably regulates for good reason the manner of communication (such as parades, loudspeakers, public signs) . If the statute has a good reason (such as keeping the streets clear for traffic, keeping neighborhoods quiet at night, or preventing ugly signs) , and the law is applied even-handedly to all, then the Court will normally approve it—unless on balance it tends unduly to inhibit people from exercising their or-dinary free speech rights.

V. Unprotected Speech

There are certain types of speech whose *content* is not protected by the First and Fourteenth amendments.

(1) *Fighting words.* During World War II, a man was arrested for calling a police officer "a damned fascist." The law under which the man was convicted was very broad. It held punishable any "offensive," "derisive," or even "annoying" words said to any person on a public street. Yet the Court found in *Chaplinski v. New Hampshire* (1942) that this law was valid because such words are likely to provoke immediate violence. Thus, those kinds of "fighting words" are not protected by the Constitution. However, a few years ago, another man was arrested for saying to a police officer, "You white son of a bitch, I'll kill you." This law was more specific than the one in *Chaplinski,* forbidding "abusive language" to another per-son in his presence "without provocation." Nevertheless, in this case, the Court overturned the conviction, stating that the law was too broad, that it could affect normal kinds of speech also. Although the Court claimed that the fighting words doctrine is still an exception to free-speech

protection, many people now wonder if there is any strength to that doctrine anymore.

(2) *Obscenity.* Obscene and pornographic words and pictures are not protected by the First and Fourteenth amendments. However, during the years Earl Warren was Chief Justice, the Court was concerned that obscenity laws might restrict controversial pieces of literature. To this end, the Justices placed so many restrictions on what would be a valid law against pornography that, in fact, there was virtually no way a state could effectively suppress obscenity. The situation has changed under the Burger Court. In the case *Miller vs. California* (1973), the Court developed what seemed to be even more specific guidelines, but which in reality allowed for greater restriction on pornography than before. Pornographic material may be made illegal if "the average person, applying contemporary community standards, would find that the work, taken as a whole, appeals to the prurient interest." The work must "describe, in a patently offensive way, sexual conduct" as precisely defined by state law, and the work, taken as a whole, must not have serious artistic, literary, or other such redeeming value. The Court emphasized that the states must define in precise detail exactly what the law forbids, and it emphasized that each different community could determine what its standard of acceptability could be. Under this approach, a number of obscenity convictions have recently been obtained, some on actors and publishers. It is not likely that this issue will soon go away, for many more appeals on the controversy will come before the Court.

(3) *Commercial speech.* During the 1940s the Supreme Court handed down a decision holding that a state could regulate commercial advertising just as it could any other economic activity. This doctrine began to come under

attack in recent cases until finally, in 1976, the Supreme Court held (in *Virginia State Board of Pharmacy v. Virginia Citizens Consumer Council*) that the state of Virginia violated the First and Fourteenth amendments by forbidding pharmacists to advertise their prices for prescriptions. The Court has now stated that commercial speech has virtually the same protection as other forms of speech. It has cut down some laws which restrict attorneys from advertising. The Court has also ruled against a city ordinance that prevents homeowners from placing "For Sale" signs in front of their houses.

VI. Press Freedom

The rights that people have in expressing themselves are the same or similar to the privileges which the press enjoys. There are a few differences, however. First of all, there is the issue of *prior restraint*. When the First Amendment to the Constitution was written, there was already a history of what freedom of the press meant in England. There it meant that there could be no censorship, no prohibition on the printing of any item. Of course *after* a statement was printed and circulated, the author could be punished if what he said had violated the law. But the author could not be prevented from publishing the article in the first place. Unfortunately in England before the American Revolution, one could be punished for saying almost anything against the King.

Here in the United States, we have kept the basic distinction between prior restraints and subsequent punishment. Almost any regulation which prevents something from being printed or said is likely to be declared invalid. Even though a state may require the licensing of any business, it cannot require licenses of publishers to print and distribute newspapers or books. (Television and radio, however, are exceptions. There, the Federal Communications Commission may validly require prior licensing, and may even regulate the content of the programming.) In *The New York Times Co. v. The United States* (Pentagon Papers Case) (1971), the executive branch had asked the federal courts to issue an injunction to prevent *The New York Times* and *The Washington Post* from publishing a top-secret analysis of the Vietnam War written by the Defense Department. The Court, by a 6 to 3 vote, upheld the right of the newspapers to publish the material even though the executive branch claimed that such publication would result in serious harm to the interests of the United States. There was no clear majority opinion, but most of the Justices said that only the most extreme emergency would justify preventing a newspaper's publishing a particular story. The case stands for the "very heavy presumption" against prior restraints in our law, but it does admit of the possibility of exceptions, particularly in a wartime emergency.

Of course when a city requires a parade permit, this too is a form of prior restraint on expression. But here the Court makes certain that the permit is only for the narrow purpose of maintaining the orderly use of the streets and cannot be used to censor anyone's ideas.

The Supreme Court has also shown another sensitivity to the freedom of the press. It consistently, with very few exceptions, has upheld the right of a publisher to print or not to print what it chooses. Even the former restrictions on printing certain kinds of advertising are beginning to fall. The Court has held that there is no "right of access" to reply to unfavorable editorials or stories either in the press or on television (unless the Federal Communications

Commission orders broadcasters to allow a right to reply). The Court has even protected the press from being sued for libel for any statements it has published (even advertisements) which criticize a political leader in the performance of his public functions. There is an exception: if the newspaper publishes a defamatory statement knowing it to be false and knowing it will cause harm, then it can be sued. But proving this sort of "actual malice" is a very difficult task.

On the other hand, the Court has refused to grant reporters the right to keep their confidential sources secret when they are testifying before a grand jury. The right of the state to require "every man's evidence" is superior, unless the state itself wishes to protect reporters by law.

Nonetheless, it is fair to say that since World War II the protections afforded freedom of speech and the press by the First and Fourteenth amendments have grown greatly in this country. In this sense, our recent history is very much unlike most of the rest of the world.

The First Amendment also states, "Congress shall make no law respecting an establishment of religion, or regulating the free exercise thereof." The first part, the *establishment clause*, has occasioned great bitterness and controversy. The original intent of the amendment's framers was to prevent the establishment of a particular sect. Some states, such as Virginia, had their own established religion, and they did not want the federal government to favor a different one. Early in our history, however, all the states gave up the idea of having any particular established religion. Today, through the Fourteenth Amendment, the prohibition against an established religion also applies to the states.

But the Court has gone much farther than the original intention of the amendment. The Court has reasoned that the true effect of the establishment clause was not merely to prevent a state-sponsored religion but to keep the state neutral as regards all religions and religious beliefs. As Justice Robert Jackson put it, the establishment clause builds a "wall of separation between church and state." That wall of separation has led the Court to ban all prayers, readings from the Bible, and other religious exercises from the public schools. This is not a question of forcing unwilling students to pray. That would be forbidden by the *free exercise of religion clause.* The Court means that the state may not sponsor a particular religion, and neither may it acknowledge God in any official capacity within the school system. This decision by the Court has been among the most unpopular, and least observed, in its history. Local school boards are constantly trying to find ways to add some legally sanctioned moments of spiritual uplift to the school day, even if they be only a period of meditation. Of course schools may have students read the Bible, but only as part of a secular course of study, such as comparative religion. One school tried to read the prayer from the Congressional Record which begins every congressional session, but the courts struck that down as well.

A state is not totally prohibited from being involved with religion. But the state's main purpose must be secular and the religious involvement only secondary. Thus a state may impose Sunday closing laws, because the Court, with rather a strained interpretation, has said that this was merely to establish a day of rest and recreation, not to favor the Christian Sabbath. Church property, like other charitable institutions, may be tax-exempt. A city may provide school bus transportation to parochial schools on the same basis as

*Church Schools Ruled Eligible
For More Public Funds
—News Item.*

public schools. A state may loan textbooks to parochial students, but not movie projectors or other like equipment. Federal grants to help construct buildings on church-related universities were upheld because the buildings were to be used for secular purposes.

Other decisions by the Court show that it has not been able to find a clear line between acceptable and improper state aid for religion-related purposes. A program which gave money for the repair and maintenance of religious schools was struck down. At the same time, a law which allowed religious schools to borrow money at low state-guaranteed rates was approved. Public schools may not allow classes in religion to be taught in the school by representatives of any faith, even if the classes are voluntary. On the other hand, schools may release students from class so that they can attend religious classes at church or temple. Congress is considering legislation to grant tax credits to parents who send their children to private school. If the law passes, there will undoubtedly be a challenge in the courts as to its constitutionality.

If the Supreme Court has not been very sensitive to the financial needs of parochial schools and students, it has had a long history of defending the right to religious choice. Indeed, freedom of religion was the earliest and most prominent right the American people fostered and protected. The classic case in which the defense of the *free exercise clause* began in earnest was *West Virginia State Board of Education v. Barnette* (1943). West Virginia required all children to salute the flag as part of the morning school exercises. But the practice violated the religious beliefs of some parents who were Jehovah's Witnesses. In 1940 in *Minersville School District v. Gobitis*, the Supreme Court had denied the Jehovah's Witness's claim, saying that a state had the right to compel flag salutes for the purpose of increasing a sense of loyalty among the children. Three years later, in *Barnette*, the Court changed its mind. The state, Justice Jackson found, had no "power to make the salute a legal duty" in the first place. The Bill of Rights took certain issues, particularly those of personal belief, "beyond the reach of majorities." The minority's religious beliefs must be protected.

In some instances, however, the state may protect the welfare of its inhabitants *against* certain practices of religious minorities. Polygamy is forbidden, even though some Mormons considered it sanctioned in their religion. One Jehovah's Witness was successfully prosecuted for violating a child labor law when her small daughter was used to help sell religious literature.

Conscientious objectors to the draft presented another set of problems for the Court. The Congress had passed an act exempting from military service those who objected to war because of sincere religious beliefs. In *United States v. Seeger* (1965), the Court held that the law also exempted those who had sincere antiwar ethics, even if they did not belong to a religion or believe in God. But in *Gillette v. United States* (1971), the Court said that a conscientious objector must show an ethical hatred of *all* wars, not just one particular war.

The Court faced one of its most difficult decisions regarding religious beliefs in *Wisconsin v. Yoder* (1972). Like many states, Wisconsin requires children to attend school until they are sixteen years old. Jonas Yoder was fourteen, and his parents refused to send him to school after the eighth grade—which he was enrolled in that year. They did this because of the requirements of their Amish faith. For that act, Jonas's parents were arrested and convicted.

Chief Justice Warren Burger held that since the state was impinging on the free exercise of the Yoders' Amish religion, the state could require school attendance only if it could show its interests to be of the "highest order." On this basis, the Chief Justice balanced the interests of the state against the interests of the Amish in the free exercise of their religion. He found first of all that the Amish belief was one of "deep religious conviction." A mere personal belief against formal education would not be enough to bring in the protections of the free exercise clause. Whether the Chief Justice realized it or not, his statement means that the Court may have to determine in future cases what is a "real religious belief," or a proper religion. This is something the Court has always wanted to avoid, for it means that the government, through its judges, is defining what is a genuine religion and what is not. This could become a very difficult problem when cases from smaller, more exotic religious sects come before the Court.

The Chief Justice also found that, to the Amish, education by the state beyond the eighth grade would conflict with their most devoutly held religious beliefs. "[E]nforcement of the State's requirement of compulsory formal education after the eighth grade would gravely endanger, if not destroy, the free exercise of the [Yoders'] religious beliefs." Furthermore, the extra year or two of public education did not add too much to what the children had already learned, especially since the Amish also give their children vocational training on their own. In these circumstances, the Chief Justice held that the Wisconsin compulsory school attendance law should not stand against the religious practices of the Amish.

What would happen if a sincere religious group believed that all formal state education violated their religion? For some members of the Court, this was an altogether different question. They left the hint that in such a case, the balance of interests may actually tip in favor of the state, even though the precious right of the free exercise of religion is involved.

The Second and Third Amendments to the Constitution, dealing with the right to bear arms and the prohibition against quartering soldiers in homes during peacetime, have not occasioned much action in the courts. The Supreme Court has ruled, however, that the right to bear arms is not related to the maintenance of a state militia. Consequently, federal laws which restrict the sales of certain kinds of firearms such as sawed-off shotguns have been upheld. After all, the National Guard (the modern name for the state militia) does not need privately owned sawed-off shotguns as part of its arsenal.

As it has worked out in our courts, the main purpose of the *Fourth Amendment* has been to give protection to a person's home. This amendment forbids unreasonable searches and seizures. It requires a search warrant in most cases. A number of rules have grown up around the search warrant rule. The warrant must be issued by a judicial officer. The police cannot issue their own warrants. The warrant must list both the place to be searched and the objects to be looked for. If other objects, not listed on the search warrant, are found during the search, they can only be used in evidence if they were in a place where those being searched for were likely to be. For example, if the police are looking for a stolen grand piano and, upon proper issuance of a search warrant, look inside a chest of drawers and find illegal drugs, the drugs cannot be used in evidence. They were not in a place where someone would hide a grand piano. The police cannot even go back to the judge and ask for a warrant to search for the drugs. What was found illegally cannot be made legal by a later use of a warrant.

When someone is arrested on the street or elsewhere outside the home, the Constitution allows a limited search of his person at that moment even without a warrant. The arrested person can be "frisked" in order to make sure he is not hiding a weapon which can be used to injure the police officer. And if other illegal objects are found on the arrested person, they can be used in evidence against him. The police may even search, without an arrest, a suspicious person if they are able to show that there is "probable cause" to believe he may be hiding something illegal and there is no time to obtain a warrant first.

If a person is arrested in his home, the police are much more limited in what they can search for without a warrant. They can search only the person himself and the area immediately within the suspect's control. In other words, the entire house cannot be searched, but only the part the arrested person could easily reach to, say, obtain a weapon or destroy evidence. Of course if someone lets the police search his home voluntarily, there is no violation of the Fourth Amendment. But the police must have strong proof that an unwarranted entrance into a home was in fact done with consent.

An automobile may be searched if the police officer has probable cause to believe that criminal evidence of illegality is within the car. In such a case, there is not enough time for the police officer to obtain a search warrant. To search a parked car, however, a police officer normally needs a warrant.

Taken together, the *Fifth and Sixth amendments* contain many protections for any person accused of a crime. The Fifth Amendment's protection against self-incrimination and the Sixth Amendment's guarantee of an attorney combined in the famous decision of *Miranda v. Arizona* (1966). Ernesto Miranda was arrested in 1963 on a charge of kidnapping and rape. His alleged victim identified Miranda as her assailant. When he was brought to the Phoenix, Arizona, police station, he was interrogated by two police officers. There was no coercion or threat of coercion. He did not ask for an attorney. After two hours of questioning, Miranda signed a confession admitting that he had committed the rape. At trial, when the prosecution put the written confession into the record, Miranda's attorney objected because Miranda had not been told that he had a right to have an attorney before signing the confession. But Miranda's attorney did not deny that the confession was made voluntarily. The trial judge agreed with the prosecutor: the confession was admitted and Miranda was convicted.

The Supreme Court found that there was no better way to protect fully a defendant's rights of silence and to have an attorney than to require the police to inform the suspect of his rights. Therefore, Chief Justice Warren said, every suspect must be told "prior to any questioning that he has the right to remain silent, that anything he says can be used against him in a court of law, that he has the right to the presence of an attorney, and that if he cannot afford an attorney one will be appointed for him prior to any questioning." There was a great deal of opposition to the *Miranda* decision. In fact, a very vigorous dissent claimed

"NOW, DO A GOOD JOB IN PROTECTING US FROM CRIME!"

that the decision represented a new and unnecessary interference with the states' abilities to form reasonable rules both for the protection of the defendant and the rights of society at large.

During the last few years, the reach of the *Miranda* decision has been cut back by the courts. The requirements of warning still remain, but not when one is a witness before a grand jury. Likewise, since the *Miranda* decision applies to conditions of police custody, the warnings do not have to be given by parole or probations officers, high school principals, private investigators, the victim himself, or even by the police when they go undercover. Putting a suspect in a lineup or obtaining blood samples or a handwriting specimen do not have to be accompanied by warnings either. If a defendant voluntarily takes the stand during his trial, the prosecution can use the defendant's confession to attack his testimony, even though the police had not given any warnings before gaining the confession. Finally, if a suspect walks into the police station house to surrender, and offers a confession, that confession will be valid and admissible in court.

The *Sixth Amendment's* guarantee to a jury trial has been before the Court frequently. In general, the Court has been able to develop relatively clear rules. To begin with, the right to a jury trial applies to all prosecutions where the defendant, if convicted, could be sent to jail for anything more than six months. The right to a jury trial does not apply to cases before a juvenile court.

In addition, the Court has long decreed that a jury must be taken from a representative cross section of the community. This does not mean that any particular jury *must* contain a certain number of blacks, women, workers, or businessmen. Rather, all that is required is that the *selection process* draw on all groups in the community. Whether a particular jury contains all classes does not matter, so long as the general pool of people from which it is drawn contains all groups. As early as 1880, the Supreme Court voided state laws which prevented blacks from serving on juries. More recently, in the case of *Taylor v. Louisiana* (1975), the Court upheld the challenge by a male defendant of a jury law which, in effect, excluded women.

As we saw earlier, the Court has been more flexible in allowing experimentation at the state level with the size of juries. It has approved a six-person jury in a Florida case, and it has allowed Oregon to convict a defendant in a noncapital case with only 10 votes out of the 12.

In 1963 the Court ruled that every person accused of a crime must have the benefit of counsel. If someone cannot afford an attorney, the state must provide for one. This right applies to felony cases, misdemeanor cases, and to juvenile proceedings. One must be allowed an attorney in preliminary proceedings, before trial, and also during police interrogation. However, there is no right of counsel to a person being placed in a lineup before he is indicted. Of course a defendant may voluntarily give up the right to counsel after he has been told of the possible consequences.

The *Seventh Amendment* requires a trial by jury in civil cases. This is a citizen's privilege when he is in federal court. The states do not have to follow this rule, unless the case involves a federal right.

The *Eighth Amendment* prohibits cruel and unusual punishments. In 1972, in the case of *Furman v. Georgia,* the Supreme Court struck down a number of state death penalty statutes because they had been applied in a seemingly arbitrary fashion, particularly against minorities. But the judges could not agree on one interpretation. Two Justices thought that the death penalty itself was cruel and unusual. The other three judges in the majority said only that the death penalty as applied in these cases was beyond what was permitted by the Eighth Amendment.

In 1976 the Supreme Court attempted to clear up the confusion. In *Woodsen v. North Carolina* the Court said that the death penalty was not by definition cruel or unusual. However, if it is applied automatically, without regard to the circumstances of the crime or of the defendant, then it can be unconstitutional. The Court stated that states must pass laws outlining the specific grounds on which a judge or jury can impose the penalty. The Court also required that the death penalty can only be imposed by a jury in a separate proceeding in which mitigating factors can be introduced.

The *Ninth Amendment* states simply that the people have other rights besides those mentioned in the first eight amendments. The Court has never applied the Ninth Amendment directly to any case. Some Justices, however, have used its language to indicate that there are rights in the due process clause of the Fourteenth Amendment which the Court can enforce. We shall discuss some of these rights in a moment.

Until the 1930s the *Tenth Amendment* was a strong protection against congressional legislation which regulated certain activities within the states. Then, for forty years, the amendment was practically a dead letter. But recently it has been resurrected again to limit congressional legislation under the commerce clause. That case, *National League of Cities v. Usery* (1976), was described earlier, in Chapter Three.

THE FOURTEENTH AMENDMENT

Besides being the means for taking most of the Bill of Rights and applying it against the states, the Fourteenth Amendment also contains many independent rights. The phrases "due process of law" and "equal protection of the laws" do not say much by themselves. But Supreme Court interpretation has transformed these phrases into powerful sources of new rights.

We know that "due process of law" guarantees fair procedure to every person who comes before a court. This is known as *procedural due process*. In addition, there are certain areas in which states may not legislate at all except under the most extreme circumstances. These protected areas are fenced off from state interference. When the Fourteenth Amendment protects these special rights, we call it a case of *substantive due process*. Substantive due process protects those *fundamental rights* the Court finds to be at the very base of our political system.

What are some of these fundamental rights? Early in this century, the Supreme Court determined that every person possessed certain economic rights. They included the right to make a contract, the right to pursue a lawful occupation, and the rights associated with owning property.

The states could interfere with those rights only if there was a need to benefit society as a whole and there was no other way to do it. The states could not interfere with those rights merely to help one group over another. For example, in *Lochner v. New York* (1905), the Supreme Court declared unconstitutional a New York law that limited to sixty the number of hours per week a baker could work. New York believed that in a bargaining process between a worker and his boss, the boss had the upper hand. To protect the worker, the state limited the hours a baker could agree to. The Court found this unacceptable. Such a law takes away the right of the bakers to contract for their labor as they see fit, the Supreme Court said. A baker has the right to contract for twenty hours, forty hours, sixty hours, or however many he wants. Being a baker is not an unusually dangerous occupation, so bakers do not need special state protection. The issue is between employee and employer. The state has no right to tell the parties what they should contract for.

Justice Holmes dissented from this decision. He said a state can pursue whatever economic policies it wants. The people elected representatives in order to have social reform. The Court should not impose its ideas of economic justice on the states.

The Supreme Court did not overturn all state laws which interfered with the marketplace. In fact, most were upheld. But the Court insisted that the state must show a larger purpose, such as the health of the people, before it would approve of such laws. Thus the Court allowed the states to limit the hours miners could work because mining was itself such a dangerous line of work. It eventually approved laws which limited the working hours of all factory workers under the same reasoning. The Court allowed maximum-hour limitations on female workers, because our society depended upon having healthy women to bear children. But at the same time, minimum-wage regulations for women were struck down. Wages did not have the same direct physical effect on women as did the number of hours on the job.

The Court used a special test, which came to be known as *strict scrutiny*, when it was studying state economic legislation. Under this test, a law would be allowed to stand only if the state could show first that there was an important governmental interest at stake, and second that there was no other practical way to accomplish what needed to be done.

As the years passed, it was evident that the United States had become a complex society. We needed new social and economic legislation to deal with difficult problems. The crisis became acute during the depression of the 1930s. At that time, the Supreme Court changed course and adopted Justice Holmes's viewpoint. No longer would economic rights be called fundamental. There would be no substantive due process protection of the right to contract. Instead, the Court allowed the states almost free rein to legislate in the economic field. The Court imposed only one condition. Any legislation must meet a *minimum rationality* or *minimum scrutiny* test. So long as there is some rational connection between the purpose of the law and the way to accomplish the purpose, then the law is valid. For example, if the state wants to protect automobile owners, it could pass a law requiring mechanics to be licensed before working on anyone's car. Is licensing mechanics a reasonable way to protect automobile owners? Of course. Is it the best way? That is irrelevant. The choice is up to the state. Any means are acceptable if they are a reasonable way to accomplish any legitimate state purpose.

Since the 1930s, the Supreme Court has applied the minimum rationality test to state economic legislation. Economic activity is no longer a fundamental right. There are, however, other fundamental rights which the Court has protected through the due process clause. Some, like free speech and freedom of religion, are taken from the Bill of Rights and placed under the protection of the Fourteenth Amendment by incorporation. Others are protected by the Fourteenth Amendment by itself. These are the rights which are the most controversial.

The greatest extension of Supreme Court power in recent years has been in the area of the right of privacy. There has been much talk about the right of privacy, but so far, the Supreme Court has not clearly developed what that right is. In some cases, the right is associated with the home, the family, and with marriage. The Court has protected the right of parents to send their children to private schools. It has struck down laws which forbade married couples to receive birth control information. It voided a law which allowed a state to sterilize habitual criminals. Sometimes the right of privacy is seen as a general right of sexual freedom. The Court struck down laws which kept contraceptives from unmarried couples and from minors. On the other hand, the Court has not yet limited state regulation of homosexual activity.

The most dramatic extension of this doctrine has been in the issue of abortion. In *Roe v. Wade* (1973), the Supreme Court declared that a woman's right of privacy included the right to have an abortion with only limited state interference. The Court devised a rule whereby during the first three months of pregnancy, there can be virtually no regulation by the state; during the second three months the state can regulate abortions only to protect the health of the woman during the operation; during the last three months, when the fetus could be born alive and survive (that is, when it is viable), the state can restrict abortions but not if the pregnancy endangers the life or health of the mother. The decision has sparked debate not only among Americans in general, but among constitutional scholars as well. Many writers approve of the result of the case, but do not find the opinion written by Justice Harry A. Blackmun as well argued.

It is difficult to find the source of this right of privacy in *Roe v. Wade*. It cannot be a right of marriage and the home, for the Supreme Court does not let parents of pregnant minors have a veto over the decision. It cannot be a right of sexual or reproductive privacy, for the Court forbids the male sexual partner, whose own reproductive rights are at stake, to have a say either. It cannot be a right of privacy of the body, for we do not allow a person to use his body freely to harm another. It must therefore be a special right of privacy associated only with pregnancy itself. Unfortunately, Justice Blackmun did not provide us with many reasons why this right is so fundamental.

Those who oppose the decision believe that it is very much like the old economic cases such as *Lochner v. New York*. They say that there is enough medical evidence for a legislature to reasonably decide that the fetus is a human and deserves some protection. A state should be able to balance the bargaining power between a worker and his boss. Likewise, the antiabortionists say, a state should have the right to strengthen the bargaining power between the unborn and the person on whom he is solely dependent.

By making abortion a fundamental right, the Court applies the strict scrutiny test to all state regulations on the subject. Few survive such a rigorous test. The Court has found that the Constitution did not regard the fetus as fully human when it was written in 1787 and that the Constitution forbids any state from defining a nonviable fetus as human now.

Whether the Court's decision is right or wrong, it shows

how dangerous it is for the Court to become involved in such emotional issues. Rather than settling the controversy, the decision has seemed to make it more acute. Finding fundamental rights in the due process clause of the Fourteenth Amendment has always been a risky business for the Court. It is the same today.

The final right we shall talk about is one which has caused great controversy and anguish in recent years. It is the right which has led the courts to order the busing of schoolchildren, the right which has led white persons such as DeFunis and Bakke to seek Court protection, the right that has voided some laws treating women differently from men. It is the important right of the Fourteenth Amendment which affirms that "No state . . . shall deny to any person within its jurisdiction the equal protection of the laws."

What does "equal protection of the laws" mean? Every law treats some people differently from others. A law which sets a speed limit treats those persons who travel over 55 miles an hour (86 kmph) differently from those who travel under the 55-miles-an-hour speed limit. Are the speeders discriminated against? Of course they are. Are they protected by the equal protection clause of the Fourteenth Amendment? Of course not. Why not? What kinds of discrimination does the equal protection clause allow? What kinds does it forbid?

The Supreme Court has developed three answers to this question. First, if the law makes ordinary distinctions between persons, the Court only applies a *minimum scrutiny* or *minimum rationality* test in the same way it does under the due process clause. If the state wants to reduce automobile accidents, is it reasonable for it to treat those who travel over 55 miles an hour differently from those who travel under 55 miles an hour. Can a state treat older people differently from younger people? Can a state give greater tax benefits to senior citizens, believing it likely they will be in greater need of income in their old age? The answer is yes to these examples and thousands more. Particularly when a state is passing economic legislation, the Court requires only a minimal rationality in the law.

What if the law differentiates between men and women? Is the same minimum scrutiny test applied? Take the case of *Craig v. Boren* (1976). Oklahoma had a law prohibiting young men between the ages of 18 and 21 from buying 3.2 percent beer. Women of the same age were allowed to purchase the beer. The state said that statistics proved that far more young men of that age than young women were arrested for drunk driving. Intoxicated drivers often kill themselves and others in the accidents they cause. To help stop this tragedy, Oklahoma restricted the sale of the beer. Under a minimum rationality test, this legislation would probably have been valid. But the Supreme Court has decided to use a tougher test in cases of sex discrimination. Sometimes called *minimum scrutiny with bite*, the test has two parts. First, the Court determines whether there is "an important governmental interest." Is the purpose of the state law important? Here the Court said that traffic safety was indeed important.

The second part of the test requires that the difference in treatment between men and women "clearly and substantially" accomplish the purpose. Does keeping only 18- to 21-year-old males from buying 3.2 percent beer (yet allowing females of the same age to buy the beer) substantially further traffic safety? Here the Court found that it did not. The difference between men and women drivers between the ages of 18 to 21 is not enough to penalize only the men. The law is therefore invalid. It violates the equal protection of the laws clause of the Fourteenth Amendment.

By a narrow 5 to 4 majority, the Court has adopted this minimum scrutiny with bite test in sex discrimination cases. Under this test, nearly all legislation disadvantaging women has been declared unconstitutional, and some legislation, as in the 3.2 percent beer case, disadvantaging men has also been declared void. There are some problems with this new test. How does the Supreme Court determine what is an "important" governmental interest? It usually has been thought that the legislature is the best body to say what is an important social policy. Also, how does the Court find out if the law clearly and substantially gets the job done? Does it use statistics? Can it measure accurately? Even if it uses statistics, how much is enough? When is something substantial and when is it not? The Court has so far given little guidance on these issues.

Finally, the Supreme Court applies the strict scrutiny test in cases of racial discrimination. This is appropriate, because the Fourteenth Amendment was drafted after the Civil War mainly to guarantee the freed slaves the full legal rights of citizenship. At first, however, the Supreme Court was reluctant to join the battle for racial equality. In the 1880s it struck down federal legislation that was similar to today's Civil Rights Acts. In 1896 in *Plessy v. Ferguson*, it approved the state policy of requiring "separate but equal" segregated facilities. During the twentieth century, the Supreme Court slowly changed its course. Step by step, it moved toward forcing states to cease disadvantaging blacks in the laws. Barriers were disallowed in graduate schools and in state universities. Finally, in *Brown v. Board of Education* (1954), the Court declared that state-imposed separation of the races was contrary to the equal protection clause. Soon all public facilities which were segregated were declared invalid.

The road to desegregation was long and torturous. It continues its troubled path. The Burger Court has dealt with the issue many times. Out of these complex cases, some rules have emerged.

First, the Fourteenth Amendment forbids only *de jure* segregation, not *de facto* segregation. *De jure* segregation means that a state or city has intentionally forced the races apart by law. This can be done by the law itself, or by the way a school board or other body applies the law. For example, if a school board draws the boundaries of school districts according to where blacks and whites live in order to keep most of the blacks in separate schools, that is *de jure* segregation. It is unconstitutional. *De facto* segregation occurs when schools have mostly white or black populations solely because blacks happen to live in one neighborhood and whites in another. If the school board has not intentionally forced the students into different schools because of their race, there is no violation of the Fourteenth Amendment.

Thus there must be an intent by the state or the school board or other body to segregate. The act separating black from white must be done on purpose. Sometimes the Court will see intent merely from the results of the law. Many years ago, in the case of *Yick Wo v. Hopkins* (1886), the Court found such a discrimination. San Francisco required that all laundries must be in a brick or stone building in order to limit the danger of fire. If someone wished to operate a laundry in a wooden building, he had to obtain a special permit. About two hundred Chinese applied for permits to have a laundry in a wooden building. All were refused. On the other hand, all except one of the non-Chinese laundries that applied for such permits were able to obtain them. The city did not try to explain the disparity. It was obvious that this was a case of racial discrimination.

The modern cases usually do not present such extreme statistics. Often one race will seem to suffer more than another from a law. But that does not mean that the law *intended* to disadvantage one race. In fact, the Court has said that statistics alone are not proof of bad intent. In such a case, the state still has an opportunity to show that it did not intend one race to suffer as a result of the operation of a law. Thus, for example, where a general aptitude test was used for selecting police recruits, the fact that proportionally more blacks than white failed the test does not mean that the test was intentionally antiblack.

Once a state or city has been found to have intentionally discriminated, it must make up for what it has done. If blacks were segregated from whites, then the courts will order that the races be mixed. If race was part of the constitutional violation, then race is part of the cure. This is why the federal courts have ordered busing, reassignment of teachers, and remedial educational programs. The courts cannot order such measures unless they have found there was previously an intentional policy of segregation.

There are limits to the cure. If one school district is guilty of segregation, a court cannot order busing of children from another innocent school district. The cure cannot be greater than the wrong. Sometimes the Supreme Court has found that a lower federal court went too far in its orders. But so long as the federal judge tailors his orders to fit what had been done unconstitutionally in the past, then the local school board must obey.

This brings us back full circle to the Bakke case. Alan Bakke had applied twice to the medical school at the University of California at Davis, but he was rejected each time. A set amount of spaces for the entering class had been reserved for minority students. As a result, blacks with lower scores had been admitted over Bakke.

In the DeFunis case, the white applicant had been turned down by the Washington State supreme court. But the California supreme court had agreed with Bakke. The court said that any time any person receives less than equal treatment because of the conscious racial intent of state law, strict scrutiny should be applied. The Washington supreme court applied strict scrutiny and still found against DeFunis. The California supreme court applied strict scrutiny and found for Bakke.

Let us recall the two parts of the strict scrutiny test. First, is there a compelling state need? Yes there is, admitted the California court. It is highly desirable that blacks and other minorities be integrated into the profession of medicine. After centuries of deprivation, a society should aid those whom it has kept out. What about the second test? Is there any other way for the university to help blacks into the profession without disadvantaging Bakke solely because he is white? There is, said the California court. Therefore, Bakke was denied his rights under the Fourteenth Amendment's equal protection clause. The court suggested that the university could have an admissions program helping disadvantaged persons of all races. It could expand the number of positions available. What it could not do was to make race the basis of choice between two applicants. Bakke had to be admitted.

The Supreme Court of the United States heard the case in the fall of 1977. The entire nation watched and waited for the decision. Would the Supreme Court face the issue of affirmative action and reverse discrimination? Or would it try to sidestep the issue as it had done in the DeFunis case?

Finally, in early July 1978, the result was announced. Four Justices, led by John Paul Stevens, declared that the University of California's admissions program violated the 1964 Civil Rights Act. Race cannot be taken into account in programs funded by the federal government. These Justices avoided the question of whether the Constitution itself permits or forbids affirmative action programs. They based their views solely on federal law.

Four other Justices, led by Justice William Brennan, asserted that the equal protection clause of the Fourteenth Amendment permitted states and state-run institutions to have affirmative racial preferences in order to remedy "the effects of past societal discrimination." Brennan went on to say that quotas were an acceptable means for such a purpose.

Justice Lewis F. Powell, Jr., cast the swing vote. As such, his opinion will be looked upon as the most important. Powell declared that "racial and ethnic distinctions of any sort are inherently suspect and thus call for the most exacting judicial examination." He said that the Constitution forbids a state agency from granting a special privilege to members of any race unless that state agency has been guilty of racial discrimination in the past. Here there was no evidence that the University of California at Davis had committed such a wrong. Therefore, it could not justify its rejection of Bakke on racial grounds.

It had been asserted by some that the Fourteenth Amendment was designed to protect minorities from laws directed against them by the majority. Blacks, for example, are a

MARGULIES

disadvantaged minority. But whites have the majority of votes in the legislature. If the majority voluntarily decides to help the minority, then the majority is not being harmed against its will. Justice Powell explicitly rejected this argument. He noted that a preference for a black person necessarily deprives a white person of a position because of his race. "The white 'majority' itself," Powell wrote, "is composed of various minority groups, most of which can lay a claim to a history of prior discrimination at the hands of state and private individuals." Powell rejected the university's argument that the goals of increasing the number of minority doctors, of redressing prior wrongs in society, and of giving greater medical care to areas which are in need of more doctors, were reason enough to prefer minorities over whites in the admissions program. No matter how compelling the goal might seem, Powell said, ". . . preferring members of any one group for no reason other than race or ethnic origin is discrimination for its own sake. This the Constitution forbids."

Justice Powell, however, left one loophole by which most affirmative action programs may be saved. He said that it was a proper objective for a university to take race into account for the purpose of seeking a more diverse student body. He emphasized that race could be counted as a "plus" so long as it wasn't the only basis on which an applicant was judged. Quotas or absolute racial preferences could not be justified. This is what the University of California had done in this case. But if a university (and here Powell cited with approval the admissions program of Harvard College) merely added race as one more factor into the mix, then such a program would be constitutional. Hence a diverse student body with a proportion of minority members may be a justifiable "goal" so long as it is not accomplished by a rigid racial quota system.

The Stevens group of Justices found this ruling a piece of *dictum,* that is, a statement of opinion unnecessary to the decision. The Brennan group of Justices could see no distinction between having a goal of a racially diverse student body and having a quota. Powell answered that he expected that universities would use good faith in seeking a diverse group of students without resorting to absolute or unfair racial preferences.

Needless to say, the Bakke case raises more questions than it answers. How can it be proven in court that a university did not use good faith in seeking to expand the number of minority members in its student body? Justice Powell stated that a university has something of a First Amendment right in the way it formulates its admissions policy. Does the same right apply to the federal government when it forces businesses and labor unions to increase minority representation in the work force? We have a long way to go in this country before we solve these agonizing racial problems. The Supreme Court has not yet made a final accounting to us in this matter.

CHAPTER FIVE

The Supreme Court at Work

When the Supreme Court announces its decisions, usually on Mondays, it states rules of law which reverberate throughout the entire nation. A conviction may be set aside; a piece of legislation voided; a desegregation plan approved. The decisions of the Court shape the law and the society far into the future.

The nine men who carry this awesome power are appointed by the President with the concurrence of two thirds of the Senate. They can be removed from office only by impeachment. They have an independence that is unmatched by any other office holders in the government.

From October to June, the Supreme Court is in session. The Justices sift through thousands of cases. Less than two hundred are argued and decided. The behind-the-scenes deliberations of the Justices are almost entirely secret. Every Friday, the Justices meet in secret conference.

"BUT THAT'S THE WAY WE DO IT HERE—
YOU EITHER AGREE WITH THE MAJORITY, OR
YOU AGREE WITH THE MINORITY."

No one else is allowed in the room. The most recently appointed Justice answers the door and takes messages. The Justices are seated around a large oak table. Each Justice has one or more carts behind him, loaded with papers, briefs, memoranda, and cases. He will need these for the day's discussion. Much of the time, the Justices decide which cases to hear. The petitions by losing parties from courts below have already been circulated to the Justices. Most Justices have their clerks ready the petitions and summarize them in separate memos. A list is made up of petitions which any Justice wishes to have discussed. None of the others are even considered by the Court.

At the meeting the Chief Justice takes the list and announces the first petition to be considered. Each Justice, in order of seniority, makes his comments. Finally the newest Justice comments and votes on whether to hear the case. The voting goes back up the seniority line, ending with the Chief Justice. If four or more Justices vote to hear the case, it is set on the docket (the list of cases) to be argued. If fewer than four vote to hear the case, the petition is dismissed. Each petition on the list is handled in this way.

The parties then submit briefs to the Court. Other interested groups can also submit briefs if the parties and Court agree. These outside parties are called *amicus curiae* (friend of the court). The number of briefs a Justice has to read for each case can be significant.

Each Justice has three or four clerks to assist him. The clerks are also sworn to secrecy. They are almost always the top graduates from the most prestigious law schools. They read the briefs, do research, prepare preliminary drafts of opinions, and discuss the cases with the Justice for whom they are working. Many of the clerks later become famous law professors, lawyers, or judges.

After the briefs are received, oral argument is set. The attorneys for each side are allowed to argue before the Court, usually for one half hour each. It can be a frightening experience for an attorney. The nine robed Justices sitting high over the attorney throw questions at him. The attorney must be able to respond with courtesy and intelligence. He must know the philosophies of each Justice, in order to make a persuasive response. Although it is not frequent, it is believed that occasionally a great oral argument has won over the Court. Normally the Justices are leaning one way or the other on the case already, based on the arguments in the briefs.

At their secret Friday conference, the Justices also consider the cases which have been argued. Starting again with the Chief Justice and the senior Associate Justice, each member puts forward his viewpoint. The viewpoints of all are heard in order, although it is likely that the discussion goes on freely around the table. Finally the vote is taken. The newest Justice votes first, while the other Justices follow up the line, with the Chief Justice voting last.

After the vote is taken, if the Chief Justice has voted with the majority, he announces which Justice shall write the opinion. If the Chief Justice is with the minority, the senior Associate Justice in the majority usually announces who shall write the opinion. The minority Justices agree among themselves who shall write the main dissent.

The drafted opinions are circulated among all the Justices. During this time, any Justice may change his vote. Sometimes a new majority is formed and the dissenting opinion is turned into the opinion of the majority. Other members of the majority may join the main opinion, seek to have it changed to reflect their views, or write their own concurring opinion. A concurrence agrees with the vote of the majority. The concurring Justice merely adds his own reasons for his vote.

When the opinions have been circulated and agreed upon they are printed and the judgment is announced, usually on the following Monday. The interpretation of the Constitution is stated anew. Frequently the law is changed. What comes down from the Court each Monday makes all of us live a little differently than we did before.

BIBLIOGRAPHY

Abraham, Henry J. *Freedom and the Court,* 3rd ed. New York: Oxford University Press, 1977.

———. *The Judiciary: The Supreme Court in the Governmental Process,* 4th ed. Boston: Allyn & Bacon, 1977.

* Barth, Alan. *Prophets with Honor: Great Dissents and Great Dissenters in the Supreme Court.* New York: Knopf, 1974.

Bickel, Alexander. *The Least Dangerous Branch: The Supreme Court at the Bar of Politics.* Indianapolis: Bobbs-Merrill, 1962.

Black, Charles L., Jr. *The People and the Court: Judicial Review in a Democracy* (reprint). Westport, Ct.: Greenwood, 1977.

Cox, Archibald. *The Role of the Supreme Court in American Government.* New York: Oxford University Press, 1976.

* Ernst, Morris. *The Great Reversals: Tales of the Supreme Court.* New York: Weybright & Talley, 1973.

Feinston, R. *Constitutional Revolution?* Cambridge, Mass.: Schenkman, 1977.

* Fribourg, Marjorie. *The Bill of Rights.* New York: Avon, 1969.

* Indicates books suitable for younger readers.

* Garraty, John A. *Quarrels That Have Shaped the Constitution.* New York: Harper & Row, 1964.

Henkin, Louis. *Foreign Affairs and the Constitution.* New York: Norton, 1975.

Jacobsohn, Gary J. *Pragmatism, Statesmanship, and the Supreme Court.* Ithaca, N.Y.: Cornell University Press, 1977.

Kurland, Philip. *Politics, the Constitution, and the Warren Court.* Chicago: University of Chicago Press, 1970.

Lusky, Louis. *By What Right?* Charlottesville, Va.: Michie, 1975.

* Schwartz, Bernard. *The Reins of Power: A Constitutional History of the United States.* New York: Hill & Wang, 1963.

Swisher, Carl B. *The Supreme Court in Modern Role.* New York: New York University Press, 1965.

ABOUT THE AUTHOR

David F. Forte holds degrees from Harvard College, the University of Manchester, England, the University of Toronto, and Columbia University School of Law. He is an associate professor of law at Cleveland State University College of Law.